Stories Jesus Still Tells

STORIES JESUS STILL TELLS

The Parables

revised second edition

JOHN CLAYPOOL

COWLEY PUBLICATIONS
Cambridge
Massachusetts

Library of Congress Cataloging-in-Publication Data:
Claypool, John.
    Stories Jesus still tells : the parables / John Claypool.
    p. cm.
    Originally published: New York : McCracken Press, c1993.
    ISBN 1-56101-185-1 (alk. paper)
    1. Jesus Christ—Parables. 2. Christian life—Anglican
    authors. 3. Spiritual life—Episcopal Church. I. Title.
BT375.3 .C53 2001
226.8'06—dc21   00-064398

Cover art: Johannes Vermeer, *Christ in the House of Martha and
Mary* (mid-seventeenth century)

This book was printed in Canada by Transcontinental Printing
on recycled, acid-free paper.

Third printing

Cowley Publications
4 Brattle St. • *Cambridge, Massachusetts 02188*
800-225-1534 • *www.cowley.org*

To my beloved wife, Ann,
without whom this volume
would not be what it is
and I would not be the person I am

CONTENTS

ACKNOWLEDGMENTS

A special word of grateful acknowledgment needs to be addressed to four individuals. The first of these is Marjorie Swanson, my esteemed colleague in ministry during all my years at Saint Luke's who patiently and lovingly typed and retyped the original drafts of the manuscript and never once complained about all the hours this project entailed. Secondly, my beloved wife, Ann, has painstakingly gone over this revision and offered literally hundreds of suggestions that have made this work superior to what it was originally. And lastly, my sincere thanks are given to Cynthia Shattuck of Cowley Publications, who initially agreed to this endeavor, and to Annie Kammerer, also of Cowley, who carefully edited the material to bring it to its present form.

PREFACE

It is enormously pleasing to me that Cowley Publications has agreed to publish a revised edition of *Stories Jesus Still Tells*. No part of the historic biblical canon has blessed me more thoroughly than the parables of our Lord. The very first sermon I ever preached, not long after making a commitment to study for the Christian ministry in February of 1949, was based on the parable of the prodigal son. Now, fifty-one years later, as I complete my service as Rector of Saint Luke's Episcopal Church in Birmingham, Alabama, my last teaching series has been a revisiting of this same genre of Holy Scripture. In the profoundest sense of the metaphor, God has "found me" most powerfully in these marvelous stories that Jesus used so redemptively in the first century, and continues to use up to the present moment.

I discovered long ago that one of the true mysteries of this world is how the printed word can find its way to people and places beyond all of our wildest imaginings. This modest attempt at interpretation is offered up to "the wind of the Spirit" to be taken wherever the mysterious One might choose. What first came as gracious gift, I now pass on in generous delight. May the "second incarnation" of this book become a helpful vehicle in Jesus' ongoing efforts to redeem all creation.

John Claypool
October, 2000

INTRODUCTION

In the long, quiet years of growing up in Nazareth, Jesus was given the task of reconciling the world back to a true understanding of the divine nature.

This was not going to be easy. Centuries before, the earliest humans had let fear take root in the deepest places in their hearts, and its presence had wreaked havoc with everything. For reasons that will never be clear, our forebears listened to a serpent's word that the Creator was not essentially good, but instead, a vicious exploiter.

Once this image of mistrust possessed their minds and hearts, humans became little more than terrified beasts. They saw threats everywhere and proceeded to unmake the lovely creation that had come from the divine hand.

Jesus, therefore, faced a major challenge. For centuries, his human brothers and sisters had operated out of a totally false perception of God, a perception that threatened to destroy God's dream of sharing his joy with the creatures of his affection. How could

God's light be shed on this dark, suspicious place in the human soul?

As Jesus pondered this challenge, a strategy from his Jewish heritage commended itself to him: the way the prophet Nathan had handled a crisis highly charged with panic and fear. Jesus recalled the story:

King David had reached the pinnacle of military and political power. In four short decades, he had risen from the obscurity of tending his father's sheep to being recognized as the most powerful figure in the whole Mediterranean basin. From the Nile to the Euphrates, David had no equal. But at this moment of unprecedented professional success, various parts of his being that he had neglected in his headlong climb to fame broke to the surface and created a personal crisis. Today we call such episodes a "mid-life crisis," a time when the imbalances created by the way one has lived need to be addressed.

In David's case, he had obviously given little attention to his own needs for intimacy. As a result, when he was pacing restlessly one afternoon on the roof of his palace—having conquered the world politically, but not having fed the hungers of his own love-starved heart—he saw a beautiful woman bathing... and suddenly he wanted her more than anything else in the world. His great success in one area had failed to satisfy other parts of his personhood. David clumsily set about to operate in the realm of love the same way he had waged war. He had the woman brought to him by force, and before the night was done he had raped another man's wife and conceived a child with her.

It is pathetic, really, to look back and see how ill-prepared David was for human relations. When he learned of the woman's pregnancy he panicked—and set in motion a major cover-up. Learning that the woman was the wife of one of his soldiers, he proceeded to manipulate regulations to send the soldier home so it would appear that the child was his. When this did not work, David had the husband sent back to the front to be killed. Then he took the beleaguered woman and made her his wife before the baby was born. This sordid drama took its toll on David. He was frenzied by guilt and panic.

Obviously, God was not at all pleased with this episode. Yet remember, David was beloved of God, "a man," the scripture says, "after God's own heart." The Holy One refused to leave David out on a limb, so to speak. He inspired the prophet Nathan to go to David as a reconciler—just as later God would send Jesus on a similar mission to the world. Then, as always, God gave Nathan a way to accomplish this delicate task. (The Holy One never sends people out to struggle on their own—God provides both the means and the end!)

Nathan knew that to confront a frightened person directly might make matters even worse. So he went to David and said, "Let me tell you a story. I want your honest opinion on something." Then he proceeded to tell him about a rich man, who owned vast properties, and one of his poor tenants, whose sole possession was a single ewe lamb that he treated as if it were a child. One day company arrived unexpectedly at the rich man's house, and instead of sending for one of his own flock, he took the tenant's lamb, had it butchered, and served it for lunch. "How do you evaluate such an action?" asked Nathan.

The king was intrigued by the story. "That rich man had no sense of justice. What he did was patently unfair. If this case were brought before me, I would pronounce him guilty and demand he repay fourfold for what he unlawfully took."

David might have thought he had rendered a final verdict, but Nathan said quietly, "David, this story is about you and what you did to Bathsheba and Uriah the Hittite." It had worked! The story, a vehicle to get behind David's defenses, enabled him to embrace the sordid truth about himself. That story marked the beginning of a whole new chapter in David's growth.

As Jesus pondered the task given to him by God, he recalled that Nathan's use of a story seemed an exceptionally effective way of doing what needed to be done. Inspired by Nathan's example, Jesus went on to perfect this methodology as no one has since. He called the stories *parables,* and they became the most distinctive form of his teaching. What the proverb was to Solomon and the fable to Aesop, these special kinds of stories were to Jesus in his mission of reconciliation.

There are certain distinctive features of this particular genre of literature:

First, the images that Jesus used in weaving these stories were always familiar and drawn from everyday life. Oftentimes modern writers make allusions that are difficult to understand. Jesus never did that. Even the most illiterate adult could identify with the situations, objects, and persons that he chose as the raw material for his parables.

Second, these stories are characterized by intriguing plots. They had a way of drawing people into the movement of the stories, which served the important purpose of lowering their defenses and opening a way for new insight to break through.

Third, perhaps the most distinctive characteristic of the parables is the element of surprise. When people thought a parable was about someone else, it turned out to be about them! Parables begin as portraits of other people, and then suddenly turn into mirrors in which people see things about themselves that they had not seen before. David found himself looking at a reflection of his own life when Nathan's parable came to its climax.

This is how Jesus worked the miracle of reconciliation again and again. People would come to him in all degrees of panic, fear, and anger. Yet instead of confronting them head-on and driving them deeper into their defensiveness, he would, like Nathan, defuse their anxiety by saying, "Let me tell you a story...." Then, drawn in by the narrative and with their defenses down, the listeners would see the story as a mirror, and its light would make their personal darkness visible.

In this way, parables became events of revelation. Profound things began to happen to people at the deepest levels of their beings. The age-old problem of fear casting out love was reversed: here was the phenomenon of love casting out fear, for human beings saw, as if for the first time, a smile on the face of their creator/redeemer. Primal trust was once again restored.

The title of this book could well have been *Nathan's Legacy*. It links the methodology Jesus used with a wisdom that goes far back in the Hebrew memory, yet remains a wisdom that is as current as this morning's newspaper. These story-events called parables have the same power to reveal us to ourselves and to show us the Father/Mother/Parent God as they did when Jesus first told them.

I invite you to open up the deep places in your being so that "the Light that enlightens every human being" can illumine you as well.

Chapter One

THE TREASURE, THE PEARL, AND THE NET

The kingdom of heaven is like treasure hidden in a field, which someone found and hid; then in his joy he goes and sells all that he has and buys that field.

Again, the kingdom of heaven is like a merchant in search of fine pearls; on finding one pearl of great value, he went and sold all that he had and bought it.

Again, the kingdom of heaven is like a net that was thrown into the sea and caught fish of every kind; when it was full, they drew it ashore, sat down, and put the good into baskets but threw out the bad. So it will be at the end of the age. The angels will come out and separate the evil from the righteous and throw them into the furnace of fire, where there will be weeping and gnashing of teeth.

MATTHEW 13:44-50

Ours is a many-splendored universe, or to use the Chinese metaphor, "a world of ten thousand things." This means, quite practically, that we are faced with a myriad of options in every direction and that we are called upon to make value judgments at every turn. Baptist minister and author Carlyle Marney used to say that there was no agony in life more acute than that experienced in those moments when we realize we have paid too much. We look at all the things we have, and consider all the sacrifices that went into their procurement, and then sense the disparity between the two. At this point, a profound sense of disappointment may settle in. I would be amazed if there is any adult who is a total stranger to such a painful experience.

We have no more fundamental task in life than facing up to the fact that there are millions of options laid out before us and that we must decide what is worth what. On the one hand, we can pay too much and confuse something that has only relative value with something that is of absolute value. On the other hand, we can not only recognize the real and the good and the truly valuable, but we can also organize our lives around such discernments. To that latter end, I am convinced Jesus told these three tiny parables of the kingdom.

Jesus chose images that were familiar to his hearers. He was not an elitist reserving his meanings for the privileged few. There was not a peasant of his day who would have had trouble understanding the stories he told.

The first of Jesus' images, the discovery of buried treasure, was not all that unusual. Many a farmer had had the experience of plowing along and suddenly hitting something, only to discover a chest full of coins or jewels or some kind of precious material. For centuries, the nation we know today as Israel had been the battleground for the two great cultures of the ancient world—the Egyptians and the Babylonians. Again and again, first one and then the other great superpower had swept across this little bridge of land.

People who had to live through such foreign invasions soon learned that the earth was the only safe place to protect their possessions. By burying things of value, it was harder for these marauding hordes to get their hands on them. Thus, when the word got out that some foreign army was approaching, the soil of Israel became pocketed with stashes of treasure. Of course, the folk who took such precautions were often killed themselves, so their treasures remained in the earth, only to be discovered accidentally by somebody else. Many of Jesus' listeners had undoubtedly had such an experience or known of someone who had happened upon a trove in this way.

I have now in my possession just such a family treasure. It consists of eight silver spoons that in and of themselves have very little value. Like all family heirlooms, however, it is the story behind the spoons that makes them so significant to me. Back in 1862, my maternal great-grandmother was living on a large plantation near Ripley, Mississippi. The Civil War was in full swing. The story is told that my forebear looked out of her upstairs window one day and in the distance saw the Union army approaching.

She ran down to the dining room and filled her apron with as much silverware as she could carry. Then she went out in the side yard, dug a shallow hole, and buried the silverware. She then turned an old wash pot over the place so the Yankees could not see the freshly dug earth. As it turned out, that silverware was about the only thing that was saved after the invaders got through their plundering. A part of the buried treasure came down to my grandmother, my mother, and then to me, and I shall always cherish these spoons.

The second of Jesus' images is the particular jewel whose value stood above all others in the first century. Diamonds had been discovered by this time, but they were so rare that they played no part in Mediterranean culture. The pearl was regarded as preeminent. Cleopatra, the Queen of the Nile, allegedly had two—one given to her by a suitor, and another supposedly worth about three million dollars in today's currency. The pearl's origin is different than that of other precious stones. A pearl develops when a grain of sand somehow gets inside the shell of an oyster and cuts the tender membrane to the quick. In reaction to this intrusion, the little organism secretes a milky-like substance to soften the sharp edges, and this takes shape around the particle of sand. In due course, someone comes along and finds the shell, opens it up, and there gleams a lovely pearl as a monument to this process of pain.

It is not surprising, then, why the ancient world valued pearls as a symbol of hope, a reminder that bad things nonetheless give birth to surprisingly good things. That imagery was not lost on the biblical writers. If you look carefully at the last book of the Bible—the Revelation to John—you will find a symbolic description of the ultimate goal of all history which is called heaven. John says the gates into this reality will be formed by this particular jewel—the well-known "pearly gates." And why is that? The symbolism is profound. We are reminded as we enter the realm of ultimate fulfillment that we do so because of the creative suffering of a God who cared about us and a Christ who came to die on our behalf. "He was wounded for our transgressions, crushed for our iniquities; upon him was the punishment that made us whole, and by his bruises we are healed" (Isaiah 53:5).

In Jesus' story, a tradesman, perhaps a veteran of many caravan journeys, came across the most exquisite pearl of them all, the loveliest he had ever seen, and responded accordingly. His eye was trained to recognize value when he saw it, and this stone prompted decisive action.

The third of Jesus' images grew out of the work of fishermen, a vocation Jesus knew quite well, for he grew up near the Sea of Galilee. These folk would set out in two boats, and when they reached the center of the lake they would let down a large net between them and pull it toward the shore. When the water became shallow enough, they would get out and drag the huge net onto the land. Then they would sit down on the bank and sort out the fish. Only those that were edible could be sold; the rest were tossed back into the water.

All three of these stories share a theme: the task of discerning what is worth what. How can we avoid paying too much for things and find the true *summum bonum,* the value of all values, the highest good of all?

In a little book called *Flux and Fidelity,* Kyle Hazelden observes that though human beings have differed widely across the ages, there are two basic drives that remain constant and are formed in every one of us. One is the drive toward self-preservation: people who are healthy want to live on. The other is the yearning to fulfill ourselves—to recognize and actualize our potential.[1] In the service of these two goals, nothing is more crucial than discerning the

10

relative values of all that we encounter. When this happens authentically, it has a way of reorganizing all of life and giving birth to new configurations of meaning.

This is certainly the implication of the first two parables. After the farmer discovered the buried treasure and the merchant found the unique pearl, their lives became genuinely different. All that they had was seen in a new light, and there was a joyful rearrangement of things. Suddenly, there was a willingness to let go of what one did have in order to acquire something that was obviously better. In other words, when the *summum bonum* comes along and is recognized, it changes the way we evaluate everything and can lead to the radical reordering of our lives. It seems clear that in these parables Jesus was addressing the whole issue of change and how it can occur in positive and creative ways.

If you stop and think about it, every experience of change has two very different aspects. On the one hand, we get something that we did not have, and on the other hand, we give up something that we did have: we gain something at the same time that we lose something. At the most basic level, this is what change is and does. In these first two parables, Jesus is saying that healthy change occurs when we discern that the thing that is being offered is greater and better than the thing that is being taken away. This is why he tells us that the man who found the treasure went and sold everything he owned to buy the field, and that he did it with great joy.

Creative changes occur in our lives when we discern that what is being given is really of a greater value that what is being asked of us. The same experience, however, becomes destructive when the gain dimension is not obvious, and when all we can think about is the loss dimension. From this perspective, change is by no means a life-enhancing and life-enriching process, but rather a diminishment and a lessening of the good.

12

I shall never forget how, not long after the death of my daughter, a wise old man said to me, "There is a relief dimension in every experience of grief." To be honest, I could not hear his meaning at the time. I was so overwhelmed by my loss that I was offended at the suggestion that there could be a gain dimension in it as well. As I lived on, however, I eventually came to see his point: in every change experience, we are being given something we did not have before. For example, I did have more time and energy to invest in my living son after his sister died, as well as more money to use for his education. This is not to say that such a rearrangement is what I would have chosen, but once the change was thrust upon me, I did have a choice. The point is that the experience of change gives us something as well as takes something away. If we can learn to focus on what we are given, then our attitude toward change can become genuinely different. Instead of digging in our heels and saying, "Come weal, come woe, my status is quo," we can begin to search through the new and different landscape which change necessarily brings for the gift that we are being given.

In the first two parables, the greater value of the new was not hard to see. The selling of all to buy what had suddenly been discovered to be more valuable was hardly a sacrifice. Neither the farmer nor the pearl merchant appear to have struggled at all, because what they were going to gain became so obvious. I want to go a step further, however, and say that even when the loss dimension seems to be enormous, I believe we can count on the fact that God will provide something that will enhance our life if only we are open to recognize it.

This conviction grows out of the trauma to which I have already referred: the death of my only daughter in 1970. Losing her was painful in every sense of the term, but it was not an event of total destructiveness. My own awareness of life as gift emerged from the agony of that bereavement and led me to the conviction that in all experiences of change, there is something of value being given. For this reason, we do not have to despair when the landscape of our lives is radically altered. There is always a basis for hope, and this prompts us to begin to search anew for the blessings that are surely hidden in every event.

Both the farmer and the merchant underwent an experience of genuine change, and in both cases the reorganization of life resulted in something even better than they had known before. In this way, Jesus invites us to process *all* changes, not just some changes, hopefully and expectantly.

However this is by no means all that these parables are meant to teach us. I see Jesus returning here to a theme that recurs throughout his teachings, an emphasis on the first commandment spoken to Moses: "I am the LORD your God, who brought you out of the land of Egypt...you shall have no other gods before me" (Exodus 20:2-3). What is the *summum bonum,* the value above all other values? Jesus called it "the kingdom of heaven," a term used interchangeably with "the kingdom of God." Exactly what is this reality? It is God, and God's kingly rule over all reality.

As subjects in this kingdom, we must never expect anything that derives its life from God to be able to meet all of our needs. Only the very fountain of all being possesses that sort of power. Augustine of Hippo expressed this understanding well when he wrote, "Thou hast made us for thyself, O God, and our hearts are restless until they rest in thee." We are, therefore, to relate to God as we relate to nothing else, and to look to the Holy One as the source of all fulfillment. The kingly rule of God consists in receiving all things from this One as a gracious gift, and then offering all things back thankfully and with the prayer, "How should all of this be used?" The gifts are then given back a second time, with the added blessing of the Holy Spirit, who imparts the wisdom we need to use the gifts of God appropriately.

Thus, "this kingly rule" is to the discerning heart exactly what the buried treasure was to the one who discovered it in the field, what the exquisite pearl was to the true connoisseur of jewels, and what the fish worth keeping were to the fishermen. Only in allegiance to God can the promise of fulfillment be realized. Ultimate attachment to anything or anyone else is called idolatry, and that is always a recipe for disappointment. Without exception, we will wind up paying too much when we put ultimate trust in that which is not God, but in one of God's creations.

How do we discern our way into recognition of what is and what is not of final worth? History suggests that most of us do it by trial and error, seeking first this and then that in an attempt to satisfy the hunger of our hearts. Years ago when I was doing some work in continuing education, I came across an old book entitled *On Loving God* by Bernard of Clairvaux, one of the foremost reformers of medieval monasticism. Bernard had observed the spiritual development of literally hundreds of monks, and out of all this exposure to folk who were intent on discovering the *summum bonum,* he came up with a fourfold continuum of successive stages toward real fulfillment. I have found this to be very helpful in understanding what Jesus was talking about in these parables.

Bernard describes stage one as "the love of self for self's sake," the infantile position that is bounded north, south, east, and west by a concern for self and self alone. This is where all of us begin the human journey. We are aware of our needs, and nothing else. The psychological term for this is "narcissism" or "egocentricity," and it does not begin to fully satisfy all the needs of the human psyche.

C. S. Lewis spoke once of being awakened in the middle of the night during his bachelor days and being unable to fall back asleep. It was totally dark and utterly still in his bedroom at Magdalen College. There was no way to perceive anything there outside himself. It was as if he were alone in a vacuous black hole. Suddenly he sat bolt upright in bed, for it dawned on him that such isolation was the logical end of a self-centered life.

"What if," he found himself asking, "we get in eternity exactly what we have lived for in time?" This means that if we have truly loved others, and beauty and ideas and causes beyond ourselves, we shall continue to participate in these realms of richness. But if we have lived only for ourselves—if every thought and concern has revolved around the self and the self alone—could it be that all we shall get will be ourselves and nothing else?

Such a condition would amount to total isolation, which is similar to that worst of all punishments, short of capital punishment: solitary confinement. Such a fate cuts across the very heart of what we human beings are and need. To be utterly and totally alone makes even the images of a burning hell seem

15

16

mild in comparison. We have no choice about beginning our lives in an entirely self-centered reality, but we do have a choice as to whether or not we remain there. Woe be to the person who ends up in the same condition of self-absorption that characterizes our beginnings. Mercifully, most folk choose to grow.

The second stage is what Bernard calls "the love of God for self's sake." Notice now that an awareness of outside realities has been born. There are other entities, yet the focus is still very much on ourselves. The goal is to turn everything around us, even God, into a means to our self-chosen ends. We love God for all that God can do for us.

The old reformer observed that stage two is about as far as the great host of humanity ever advances in its religious development. Individuals are aware of God, but they are intent on using the Holy One to fulfill their own agendas.

If we are at all honest, we can recognize ourselves at least some of the time in this second stage. Look for a moment at the shape of your prayers. Are they not filled with personal requests and even demands? "Give me this...protect me from that...grant me the desires of my heart."

I once knew a woman who lost a child to a serious illness. She had tried her best to get God somehow to intervene and heal her beloved one. When that did not occur, she responded in rage and bitterness. When she could not get God to jump through her hoops on her own schedule, she promptly broke off all diplomatic relations with the Holy One and became an angry cynic. This is what often comes of "the love of God for self's sake" simply because "God's ways are not our ways, nor are God's thoughts our thoughts." God is not, finally, a cosmic bellhop who responds dutifully to our commands.

Although this stage represents progress over infantile narcissism, it remains a manipulative, utilitarian approach to God, and ultimately will not really satisfy all the needs of our heart.

Bernard's third stage represents a quantum leap forward. He calls it "the love of God for God's sake." This is when one senses that God has value, not just in terms of what God can do for us, but in terms of what God intrinsically is. There are reasons to worship God that have nothing to do with our needs, but only with the wonder of what God is. Here is the beginning of ecstasy and wonder, the kind of disinterestedness that develops when we finally get ourselves off our hands and exude joy. God did not have to be the way God is; that such a wonder of Being does exist becomes the focus of one's delight.

One of my loveliest memories goes back to the time when my little girl was about four years old. I was hard at work in my study one morning when she quietly slipped in—still in her night clothes—and without a word, climbed up in my lap and laid her head on my shoulder.

"I'm really glad to see you," I said to her. "What can I do for you? What do you want?"

She paused for a moment and then said, "Nothing. I just wanted to be close to you, that's all."

The memory of that moment is still golden to me, for she was not there on any utilitarian mission—just the wonder of being with and sharing! That experience gave me such satisfaction that it pains me to realize how few times I have gone into God's presence in that spirit—without any purpose except to say, "I simply want to be with you and glory in what you are, not in what you do for me." This statement reflects "the love of God for God's sake," and if I had been ordering the stages of fulfillment instead of Bernard, I would have made this the ultimate level. If we could ever get out of ourselves long enough to love God solely for what God is, that, in my view, would be the pinnacle of all our spiritual strivings.

Therefore, imagine my surprise when I found that the wise reformer conceived a fourth stage above "the love of God for God's sake." Do you know what it was? "The love of self for God's sake." I was shocked at first, but as I began to reflect, I realized the wisdom of this profound man. Think about it for a moment. Who is the most difficult person in the world for you to love? Whom do you have the most trouble accepting, affirming, celebrating, and then embracing?

If your experience is anything like mine, you would have to admit that it is yourself. One of my deepest issues with God goes back to the very first thing God did for me—namely, create me. For some reason, the body I have, the mind I was given, the family system into which I was born—none of these is easy for me to affirm. There is much about my very being that I simply do not like, and in this sense, I do not feel I am alone.

Across the years I have probably asked a hundred people in counseling sessions the same question: "Are you talented?" And I have yet to have one person respond with an unequivocal "Yes!" "Oh, no, I was behind the door when they passed out the gifts," they would rather say. "I have no talents, really." Folk may see this as a form of humility, but the truth is that it is blatant self-dislike, and it lies at the bottom of our relationship to God. We do not seem to believe that God really knew what God was doing when he created us.

I remember so well how this negative sense of self dominated my early childhood. I would sit on the front porch back in the 1930s and daydream. I remember wishing that I was tall and thin with straight black hair, and that my name was Dick. These were very real childhood desires, and do you realize what they imply? I did not like the way I had come up from "the gates of the morning"; that is, being a short and stocky boy named John with wavy brown hair. I did not regard the way I had come into history as something good.

Thus, Bernard was right when he designated "the love of self for God's sake" as the highest stage of spiritual development. As I have said earlier, being able to regard our own creation the way Genesis says God regards it—as something "good, good, very, very good"—is the essence of Christian redemption. What this means in these parables is that each one of us, by virtue of being created by God, is the treasure buried in the field, the pearl of great price, and the fish valuable enough to keep.

Thus, the way to fulfillment lies in affirming that what God did in creation was good and in letting that become *our* joy, as surely as the farmer, the pearl merchant, and the fishermen found their joy in what they discovered. Given that most of us have felt negatively about ourselves, finding out how God feels about us may be the most surprising discovery we will ever make.

The last words of the parable describing the end of the age are ominous indeed. They warn that the angels will come and separate the evil from the righteous, and throw the evil into a furnace of fire where they shall weep and gnash their teeth forever. Why did Jesus include this word of fearful judgment? To explain that our existence is a decisive affair. It is possible to come to the *summum bonum* and to be fulfilled. It is also possible to miss the point altogether, and come to an ultimate failure. However, we must never forget that the purpose behind judgment is growth, not condemnation. God judges us in order to teach us something, not to blow the whistle on us forever.

I have long felt that God's judgment is more like a flower show than a police court. In the latter, the focus is on guilt and punishment, while in the former, the goal is learning more about moving toward perfection.

One of my cousins excelled in flower arranging. She used to enter shows, not to be condemned or exonerated, but to let the judges teach her what they knew about the ideal. This is how I imagine God's judgment. Remember, it is not God's will that any should perish, but rather that all shall come to the joy of fulfillment. Therefore, God will do everything possible to bring each one of us to this goal—but not even an omnipotent God can coerce us into such a reality against our wills. This is why I said that ours is a decisive existence.

C. S. Lewis is right, I believe, when he says that there will come a time in the Great-Not-Yet when either we will say to God, "Thy will be done," and enter into the joy of the Lord, or God will say with infinite sadness to us, "Thy will be done," and let us go back into the nothingness from whence we came.[2] If we do not receive the gift of God's love, it cannot be injected into us like penicillin. Thus, all these seemingly dark sayings about the End Time are not put there because God is a sadist about to explode in rage. They are a monument to human freedom, and reminders that finally you and I have to decide about what God has already decided—namely, that we are

invited to share God's joy. If we steadfastly refuse to
say yes to the invitation, no one in all the universe
will be sadder than God. Nonetheless, the joy God
sets before us can only be received, it cannot be
forced on a creature.

Some years ago I had a vivid dream. I had been
reading Raymond Moody's small book *Life After
Life,* which is a collection of several people's accounts
of near-death experiences.[3] This undoubtedly was at
work in my subconscious and shaped the images I
experienced. I dreamed I died physically, moved
through a dark tunnel, and came out into what can
best be described as "kindly light." There was no visible object or figure, only a great sense of warmth and
acceptance. Then a Voice said, "Welcome, my child. I
want to ask you some questions."

I stiffened in fright and thought to myself, "Here
comes the judgment and my condemnation."

But the Voice said, "First, I want to ask you, can
you weep over all the mistakes you made, over all the
pain you have caused other people, over all the ways
you have failed to live up to your highest and best?"

I began to think about the many things in my life
that were occasions for regret. Genuine tears began
to come up from the depths of my being, and I cried
as if my heart would break.

But then the Voice spoke again. "Let me ask you
something else. Can you laugh over all the good
experiences you have had, all the good jokes you
have heard, all the funny things you have seen?"

Again, I began to remember back over all the joys
of my life and started laughing as I had never
laughed before, and so help me, it seemed that that
ocean of light was laughing with me! If you have
never heard the laughter of God, you have missed
something absolutely ecstatic.

Then the Voice spoke yet again. "I need to ask you one more question. This wonder of aliveness—do you want any more of it? Do you want to go on living?"

I remember thinking that there was no predestined answer: I really did have a choice. I pondered slowly all the pain and pleasure that I had known from living, and then from the deepest place in my being I said, "Yes! Yes, I do want some more of it!"

With that the Voice exclaimed delightedly, "Come, then, you blessed of the Father, and enter into the joy of your Lord. Plunge deeper in and further on," and with that I swam off into the ocean of light.

I do not claim for this dream any ultimate authority, but I do believe it corresponds to the highest and deepest notes of the Christian vision. To enter the kingdom of heaven, what could be more essential than being able to weep over our sins, to laugh appreciatively over all our good times, and to say from the depths of our beings, "Yes, Lord, I want more of it." That would be "loving self for God's sake," would it not? It represents the *summum bonum* about which these parables speak.

In God's eyes, we are all a treasure, a pearl of great price, a keeper!

In our own eyes, I wonder, how do we see ourselves?

Chapter Two

THE VINEYARD OWNER AND HIS WORKERS

For the kingdom of heaven is like a landowner who went out early in the morning to hire laborers for his vineyard. After agreeing with the laborers for the usual daily wage, he sent them into his vineyard. When he went out about nine o'clock, he saw others standing idle in the marketplace; and he said to them, "You also go into the vineyard, and I will pay you whatever is right." So they went. When he went out again about noon and about three o'clock, he did the same. And about five o'clock he went out and found others standing around; and he said to them, "Why are you standing here idle all day?" They said to him, "Because no one has hired us." He said to them, "You also go into the vineyard." When evening came, the owner of the vineyard said to his manager, "Call the laborers and give them their pay, beginning with the last, and then going to

24

*the first." When those hired about five o'clock
came, each of them received the usual daily wage.
Now when the first came, they thought they would
receive more; but each of them also received the
usual daily wage. And when they received it, they
grumbled against the landowner, saying, "These
last worked only one hour, and you have made
them equal to us who have borne the burden of the
day and the scorching heat." But he replied to one
of them, "Friend, I am doing you no wrong; did
you not agree with me for the usual daily wage?
Take what belongs to you and go; I choose to give
to this last the same as I give to you. Am I not
allowed to do what I choose with what belongs to
me? Or are you envious because I am generous?"
So the last will be first, and the first will be last.*

MATTHEW 20:1-16

The setting of this parable was quite familiar to
first-century Palestinians. It was the harvest season for a grape crop. The owner of a vineyard got up
before dawn and went to the center of the village
where day-laborers congregated, hoping to find
employment for the twelve-hour workday. These
were the folk who did not have regular jobs, nor did
they own any property. They were much like the
migrant workers of our day; that is, they were totally at the mercy of others for any sort of employment.

Let me pause to note that most of us have a deep
aversion to this kind of powerlessness. In a profound
sense, however, these individuals mirror the condition of each one of us in relation to life itself. In the
basic structure of things, we are all beings who were
called into existence by a power other than ourselves,
and we live each moment by the grace and generosity
of that One who wanted us to be. None of us willed

our way into this existence, nor set in motion the process that called us out of nothing into being.

We are also radically dependent by nature. The English word "dependent" comes from the Latin word meaning "to hang." We human beings depend like a chandelier, hanging, held in place by something other than itself. Should that something ever let go, it has no power in and of itself to avoid crashing down into brokenness. Such an image, however, need not depress us. The essence of Christian salvation lies in learning to trust that Greater Than Ourselves on whom we depend. I once heard author Carlyle Marney say, "When I die, I am going to get to the place where I will have to say, 'If there is anything more, it is up to God. I have no power to make anything else happen.'"

This, of course, is radical dependence. To those who have learned to trust, however, such recognition need not bring on an experience of despair. If Jesus taught us anything at all, it is that when we get to the end of our ropes, we are not at the end of everything. There is Another at that point of utter extremity, and that other one is good! In this light, dependence ceases to be a threat and becomes a comfort. But let us get back to our story.

When the vineyard owner arrived, he chose only a select few of those assembled to go to his field. For the sake of illustration, let us suppose that thirty of these day-laborers were standing there. He picked out six and agreed to pay them the going wage, a denarius, which was about enough to keep a peasant family going for a single day. Notice carefully that an injustice of sorts was done here, for thirty were available and only six were hired. Yet you hear no word of protest from the chosen ones at this juncture. They were more than pleased to have a whole day's work ahead of them and the promise of taking home something to their families in the evening.

This underlines the fact that our sense of justice is often highly subjective. Most of us never complain about injustice when it falls in our favor. In the game of poker, the player who has four aces rarely calls for a re-deal. Do you ever remember someone in such a situation saying, "Look, this isn't fair. I have this incredible hand! Let's reshuffle and start all over." That is not the way human nature works, and I am intentionally emphasizing this point, for those who became most upset at the end of the day had no complaints when things were breaking in their favor.

As the story unfolds, when the vineyard owner returned at nine o'clock in the morning and found a pool of laborers still standing in the square, he told six more of these men to go to his vineyard and promised to pay them an appropriate wage. At twelve noon and then at three o'clock in the afternoon he did the same thing, and at five that evening, just one hour before the workday was to come to an end, the vineyard owner went back to the village square and encountered what has to be a minor miracle, if you stop to think about it. Amazingly, there were still six day-laborers waiting, hoping against hope that they could get some kind of work so that they could put something on the table for their families. People with less courage and tenacity would have given up long before in despair, but here were individuals who had waited in hope for eleven interminable hours.

The vineyard owner asked, "Why are you still here? Is it because you are lazy and do not want to work?"

"No, sir," they answered, "we're here because nobody has been willing to hire us."

"Go to my vineyard, then, and I will pay you what is appropriate and just."

Please note that at this point in the parable, everybody is partially satisfied, for each one had received at least a portion of what he had wanted before the rising of the sun. None was going to have to go home empty-handed to a houseful of hungry children.

Then, at the close of the work day, the vineyard owner instructed his steward to call in all the laborers and said, "Pay those who have worked the least amount of time first and then pay the rest."

When these men who had worked just an hour came up to the paying station, they were given, to their astonishment, a whole denarius, the going wage for twelve hours' work. Needless to say, they were delighted. When the three o'clock group came in, they too were given a whole denarius, as were the noon, the nine A.M., and the six A.M. groups. However, at this point, all hell broke loose. Those who had been hired first were livid and demanded an audience with the vineyard owner.

To his credit, the vineyard owner did not hide behind his steward and let somebody else do his dirty work for him. He replied, "Listen, there has been no injustice here. I've paid you exactly what I agreed to pay you at six this morning."

Then he added an interesting note. "Am I not free to do with my abundance what I want? Or do you begrudge me my generosity?" Deeper than the issues of justice or fairness, this is the pivotal point of the whole story.

The first time I read this parable, I must admit it struck me as being rampantly unfair. I found myself saying, "But that is not just!" After some reflection, it dawned on me that I was starting at the wrong place. If you and I had earned our way into this world or had received our existence as some sort of entitlement, then there might be validity to such a complaint. But the beginning point of this parable is *grace,* not entitlement, and the same is true of life as well. Birth is windfall, and life is gift. We were called out of nothing into being in an astonishing act of generosity for which we can claim no right. Once that gift becomes our central focus, it changes forever how we interpret things. If entitlement is our vantage point, we evaluate the particulars of our lives from that perspective. On the other hand, if grace is our starting point, everything begins to appear in a very different light.

There is another Jewish parable that both parallels and illumines Jesus' story, and it has helped to clarify my understanding greatly. This one is about a farmer who lived in Poland. For generations before him, his family had been very poor. One night he was awakened by an angel of the Lord, who said: "You have found favor in the eyes of your Maker. He wants to do for you what he did for your ancestor Abraham. He wants to bless you. Therefore, make any three requests that you will of God, and he will be pleased to give them to you. There is only one condition: your neighbor will get a double portion of everything that is bequeathed to you."

The farmer was startled by this revelation and woke up his wife to tell her all about it. She suggested that they put the whole thing to a test. So they prayed. "Oh, blessed God, if we could just have a herd of a thousand cattle, that would enable us to break out of the poverty in which we have lived for generations. That would be wonderful." No sooner had they said these words than they heard the sound of animal noises outside. Lo and behold, all around the house were a thousand magnificent animals!

During the next two days, the farmer's feet hardly touched the ground. He divided his time between praising God for such great generosity and beginning to make practical provisions for his newly acquired affluence. On the third afternoon, he was up on a hill behind his house trying to decide where to build a new barn when he looked across at his neighbor's field, and there standing on the green hillside were two thousand magnificent cattle. For the first time since the angel of the Lord had appeared, the joy within him evaporated and a scowl of envy took its place. He went home that evening in a foul mood, refused to eat supper, and went to bed in an absolute rage. He could not fall asleep because every time he closed his eyes, all he could see were his neighbor's two thousand cattle.

Deep in the night, however, he remembered that the angel had said he could make three wishes. With that, he shifted his focus away from his neighbor and back to his own situation, and the old joy quickly returned. Digging deep into his own heart to find out what else he really wanted, he began to realize that in addition to some kind of material security, he had always wanted descendants to carry his name into the future. So he prayed a second time: "Gracious God, if it please thee, give me a child that I may have descendants." With that, he and his wife made love, and because of his experience with the cattle, he was not too surprised shortly thereafter to learn that she was expecting.

The next months were passed in unbroken joy. The farmer was busy assimilating his newly acquired affluence and looking forward to the great grace of becoming a parent. On the night his first child was born, he was absolutely overjoyed. The next day was the sabbath. He went to the synagogue, and at the time of the prayers of the people, he stood up and shared with the gathered community his great good fortune: now at last a child had been born into their home. He had hardly sat down, however, when his neighbor got up and said, "God has indeed been gracious to our little community. I had twin sons born last night. Thanks be to God." On hearing that, the farmer went home in an utterly different mood than the one in which he came. Instead of being joyful, once again he was filled with the canker of jealousy.

This time, however, his envy did not abate. Late that evening, he made his third request of God: "Please, gouge out my right eye."

No sooner had he said these words than the angel who had initiated the whole process appeared again and asked, "Why, son of Abraham, have you turned to such vengeful desirings?"

With pent-up rage, the farmer replied, "I cannot stand to see my neighbor prosper. I'll gladly sacrifice half of my vision for the satisfaction of knowing that he will never be able to look on what he has."

Those words were followed by a long silence, and as the farmer looked, he saw tears forming in the eyes of the angel. "Why, O son of Abraham, have you turned an occasion for blessing into a time of hurting? Your third request will not be granted, not because the Lord lacks integrity, but because God is full of mercy. However, know this, O foolish one, you have brought sadness not only to yourself, but to the very heart of God."

Do you see the parallel between the two parables? In both cases, some individuals had nothing, knew themselves to be powerless and undeserving, and then, out of the blue, grace came cascading into their lives. As long as they stayed focused on what had been given to *them,* their experience was one of incredible joy. In both cases, however, what had at first been the occasion of great celebration turned into something very different, because it was subjected to the sidelong glance of envy. Some folk began to compare what they had to what *others* had, rather than to what was theirs at the outset, and in both parables their joy turned into curdled bitterness.

If you want to be miserable, then compare what you have to what some others have. Invariably, there will be someone who has done better than you, who may not have worked as hard yet wound up with a better outcome. If you base your evaluating on the sidelong comparative angle, I guarantee that it will always wind up making you miserable. In the whole process of evaluation, the selection of criteria is absolutely crucial.

You may have heard about the man who went to work on Monday morning and ritualistically asked his boss, "How is your wife?" He was startled when the boss shot back, "Compared to what?" One does not have to be a philosopher to realize that this second question really is basic. You see, compared to Marilyn Monroe, the boss would have answered the question one way. Compared to Mother Theresa, the response would have been altogether different. Any kind of interpretation hinges on the criterion you choose, and this is the crucial meaning that Jesus was trying to convey. If I compare what I had before December 15, 1930, when I was born, then all the particulars of my life look wonderful in relation to the nothing I was before birth. This body, this mind, this place in history—they are a windfall in relation to not having the chance to be at all. If, however, I begin comparing my body to Arnold Schwarzenegger's or my mind to Stephen Hawking's or my wealth to Bill Gates's, what I am and what I have begin to look utterly different. Hence, a fail-safe recipe for joy is regarding our life as a gift. A fail-safe recipe for misery is comparing our lot to someone else's and forgetting what a grace life really is.

I have a minister friend who told about a wonderful family in his parish. They already had four children and awaited with delight the coming of a fifth child. Everyone gathered at the hospital the night she was born. She was perfect in every way except one—for some reason she had no arms and no legs. The doctor could not account for this genetic abnormality. This was a family of great resilience and courage, however, so instead of spending a lot of energy feeling sorry for themselves, they took this little girl as she was born and set out to give her every advantage they possibly could under the circumstances. She lived to be twenty-one, and my minister friend said that she developed into one of the most scintillating and delightful human beings he had ever known. She had a brilliant mind, a wonderful sense of humor, and a great capacity for friendship, although never once in her twenty-one years was she able to dress or feed herself, or do any of the things most of us tend to take for granted.

One Easter her older brother brought his roommate home from college for the weekend. A philosophy major, and a sophomore to boot, he was in the habit of putting life under a microscope and analyzing everything critically. After witnessing this girl's life for three days, he asked her, "What keeps you from blowing up in anger at whatever kind of God would have let you be born into this world in this condition? How do you keep from being a volcano of resentment?"

This young woman looked him dead in the eyes and said, "I realize that compared to what most people have, what I have does not seem like much. But listen, I have been able to see and hear. I've been able to smell and taste and feel. I have been exposed to some of the world's great literature and heard some of the finest music ever composed. I've had some of the most wonderful friendships that anybody could ever have. I know what I have does not seem like much when compared to what other people have, but when compared to never getting to be at all, I would not have missed being born for anything!"

Where did this human being get the courage to pick up this kind of hand and play it with such relish? Somewhere along the line, someone had taught her that life is gift and birth is windfall, and that when compared to not getting to be at all, simply being born is better than winning the Irish Sweepstakes. If you want a formula for making the best of the less-than-perfect and making the most of what you have been given, then begin to compare your lot to what you were before you were born, and it will empower you with wonder every time. In Jesus' parable, every one of the workers had an occasion for gratitude if they had only remembered what their circumstances were like before dawn.

The vineyard owner also points the way to human potential. In the end he was not a perpetrator of injustice, but rather a model of how wealth can be used compassionately and creatively. What he did for the last four groups of workers was motivated by sensitivity and concern, not abstract justice. He realized that all thirty of those men had families to feed and needed a whole denarius. He was thinking about them, not the service he had received from them, in deciding to pay them as he did. It was his generosity—not just the concept of fairness—that accounts for his action, and we would do well to learn from him and do likewise.

This virtue is illustrated beautifully in another Jewish parable about a father and two sons. The father was an ideal mentor. He took his boys to the fields as soon as they were big enough to walk and taught them all he knew about farming. When he died, instead of dividing their inheritance they continued to work together in partnership, each contributing his best gifts and dividing every harvest down the middle. One of the brothers married and had eight children; the other remained a bachelor.

One night, during a particularly bountiful harvest, the bachelor brother thought to himself, "My brother has ten mouths to feed and I have only one. He really needs more of this harvest than I do. However, I know him. He is much too fair to renegotiate our agreement. I know what I will do. I'll take some of my harvest and slip it over in his barn at night so he can have more for his family."

At the very same time, the married brother was thinking to himself, "God has blessed me with this fine family. My children will take care of us when I am old. My brother is not as fortunate. He really needs more of this harvest to provide for his old age, but I know him. He is far too fair to renegotiate our agreement. I know what I will do. I'll take some of my harvest and slip it into his barn to build up a nest egg for the future."

As you might have anticipated, one night when the moon was full these brothers came face-to-face, each on a mission of generosity. The old rabbi said that although there was not a cloud in the sky, a gentle rain began to fall. Do you know what it was? It was God weeping for joy because two of his children had gotten the point. The real secret of human joy is in sharing what we have with others rather than hoarding everything for ourselves.

I imagine the same God wept for joy over the actions of the vineyard owner that late afternoon. He, too, modeled what it means to be made in the image of a generous God—and the truth is that we are all chips off that same beloved Block!

35

Chapter Three

THE TALENTS

For it as if a man, going on a journey, summoned his slaves and entrusted his property to them; to one he gave five talents, to another two, to another one, to each according to his ability. Then he went away. The one who had received the five talents went off at once and traded with them, and made five more talents. In the same way, the one who had the two talents made two more talents. But the one who had received the one talent went off and dug a hole in the ground and hid his master's money.

After a long time the master of those slaves came and settled accounts with them. Then the one who had received the five talents came forward, bringing five more talents , saying, "Master, you handed over to me five talents; see, I have made five more talents." His master said to him, "Well done, good and trustworthy slave; you have been trustworthy in a few things, I will put you in charge of many things; enter into the joy of your master." And the one with the two talents also came forward saying,

"Master, you handed over to me two talents; see, I have made two more talents." His master said to him, "Well done, good and trustworthy slave; you have been trustworthy in a few things, I will put you in charge of many things; enter into the joy of your master." Then the one who had received the one talent also came forward, saying, "Master, I knew that you were a harsh man, reaping where you did not sow, and gathering where you did not scatter seed; so I was afraid, and I went and hid your talent in the ground. Here you have what is yours."

But his master replied, "You wicked and lazy slave! You knew, did you, that I reap where I did not sow, and gather where I did not scatter? Then you ought to have invested my money with the bankers, and on my return I would have received what was my own with interest. So take the talent from him, and give it to the one with the ten talents. For to all those who have, more will be given, and they will have an abundance; but from those who have nothing, even what they have will be taken away. As for this worthless slave, throw him into the outer darkness, where there will be weeping and gnashing of teeth."

MATTHEW 25:14-30

A talent was originally a unit of measurement, like a gram or an ounce of precious metal, and in Jesus' story, this is the way the word is used. But the parable has become so well known to English-speaking people that the word "talent" has come to mean any capacity or ability that a human being has received from God. We no longer think of a talent as just a unit of gold or silver: instead, we talk about musical talent, artistic talent, athletic talent. I point this out simply to remind us of the enormous influence that this story has had on the shaping of our Western understanding of reality. Its images speak directly to our era of human history. Therefore, let us look at the story carefully to see where we can find ourselves reflected in it and discover some resources for our own growth. Here is how Jesus began.

The people to whom Jesus first spoke these words were very familiar with a practice of this sort. In those days, wealthy people fell into two groups, merchants and rulers. The merchants had to journey to other places to secure their goods, some going as far as India and parts of southern Europe; and the provincial rulers in the system of the Roman Empire, mostly tax collectors, were summoned to Rome from time to time. Before departing on long journeys, merchants and rulers turned over their property to trusted slaves. Because travel was so uncertain back then, there was no way of knowing how long they would be gone or if they would ever come back at all.

One example of this scenario involved the son of Herod the Great, a man named Archelaus. In 4 B.C. a shift of imperial power occurred, and he had to return to Rome to secure his right to continue the oversight of Judea and Samaria. In the custom of the day, he called his most trusted lieutenants and made each one of them responsible for certain parts of his holdings. He would have charged them to do what they had seen him doing, and to be ready to give an accounting when he returned.

Incidentally, there is a funny side to Archeleaus's particular situation. He had created quite a few enemies, as all rulers are likely to do. Thus, when he went to Rome to secure his claim on the future, fifty Jews also went to the Emperor to protest his fitness as a ruler and to ask that another be appointed in his place. When the Emperor ruled in favor of Archelaus, those fifty folk wisely decided not to return home. In other words, they had left their property under someone else's control and never returned to see what had been done with it.

Not only is such an image reflective of the way things were done in that era, but it also describes accurately the way the Hebrews understood the relation of God to history and to human beings. Creation was originally an act of divine generosity: the Holy One set out to enable creatures in his own image to experience the kind of joy that was uniquely God's. This meant that such beings would necessarily have to possess three characteristics, if the divine goal were to be achieved. They would need power—the ability to do things, to make things happen. They would need freedom, for no robot could experience God's kind of personal ecstasy. And they would need the quality of spirit that God possesses, one that finds delight in doing those things that both please the actor and bless all who are affected by such actions. God's particular kind of joy is made up of these three components, and they determine the specific way God relates to human creatures.

Geddes MacGregor has written a wonderful little book entitled *He Who Lets Us Be*. His premise is that God shows his love for us as much in what he does *not* do for us as in what he does do. He says if our understanding of divine compassion is one in which God always hovers over us like a mother over an infant, then we are only seeing one aspect of God's reality. MacGregor quotes with great appreciation Simone Weil's well-known dictum, "Creation was the moment when God ceased to be everything so we humans could become something."[1]

40

In other words, for human beings to develop fully, God must back away from us and allow us to move on our own. How would a baby ever learn to walk if her parents continued to carry her everywhere? By putting the child down and moving away, the possibility of personal growth begins. Thus, God's self-distancing from us is not a sign of desertion or abandonment, but precisely an expression of a love that wills us to grow. This is how the Hebrews understood the dynamics of creation, and it corresponds beautifully with Jesus' analogy of a rich man handing over certain powers and freedoms and then going away. When God ceased to be the sole actor on the stage of history, our chance to become actors as well was born. It is God's plan, then, that we grow up under a loving eye but not under a domineering thumb. This is the framework Jesus sets forth in the parable to describe God's relation to us and our relation to God.

But the story continues to unfold. One slave was entrusted with five talents, another with two, and the third with only one, each according to his ability. Here is yet another accurate reflection of our human condition. Søren Kierkegaard, a Danish philosopher who was much given to paradox, once observed that we humans are at once "exactly alike and utterly different." He insisted that one must hold both of those ideas together simultaneously or the uniqueness of our human situation will become distorted. I think this is correct, although it is never easy to embrace at one time what seems on the surface to be contradictory.

Years ago, when I was in graduate school and reading a lot of Kierkegaard, I was flying on a plane with an old professor, and we were discussing this very issue. "Isn't paradox," I asked, "the basic form of all finite knowledge?" He looked out the window for a long time, and then he replied, "Yes and no!"

His answer, of course, confirmed my point. Yet how can we humans be exactly alike and at the same time utterly different? Look for a moment at these three individuals whom Jesus identifies in this parable. There is a sense in which each one of them is exactly alike, in that each received his opportunity because of the action of another. None of these individuals possessed anything of their own. What they had was bequeathed to them by this owner.

By the same token, each one of them was given the same mandate: they were to imitate what they had seen the master doing while he was with them. They were to perpetuate the process that he had set in motion. Each one was also told that when the owner came back, they would be accountable for what was entrusted to them. In these ways all three were exactly alike. And truth be told, the same can be said about all of us.

Every one of us was given our chance to live by the action of Another. We did not engineer our birth into the world. It was a gift—a sheer, total, and unmerited gift. We were all given the same mandate as well: to do with our gifts and powers what God does with his. And the note of accountability also applies to each one of us. God is not an irresponsible or indifferent giver. God is going to want to know at the end of our journey what we have done with all we were given in the beginning through the abundance of divine generosity. It is in these ways that we humans are all just alike.

At the same time, these three were also markedly different from each other: one had responsibility for five talents, another for two, and another for only one. Once more, this is an accurate reflection of our human situation: while we are alike in our relation to and dependency on God, we are very different in terms of our natural capabilities and backgrounds, and the opportunities that are open to us. Humankind has not been created equal in this regard.

There was an African-American man who worked for my grandfather all his life on a farm in Kentucky. I am not sure he had more than a third-grade education. He used to pride himself on having been born on the same day and year as Franklin Delano Roosevelt. I used to hear him brag about his similarity to our revered President, but what a difference of opportunities opened out before those two individuals who entered history at the same moment!

Now let us reflect upon the way these three slaves responded to their challenges. The one who had received five talents went out at once and put these resources to work, just as his mentor had always done. Before long he had turned the five talents into ten. The one who had received the two talents did exactly the same thing, but the slave who received only one talent responded in a very different fashion. He dug a hole in the ground and buried his master's money.

After a considerable period, the landowner returned to settle all accounts. When the five-talent man went forward bringing five talents more, the landowner exclaimed, "Well done, good and trustworthy slave!" I hear in this an echo from the first chapter of Genesis, where God looked on what he had done and exclaimed, "It is good! It is good! It is very, very good!" The master continued, "You have been trustworthy in a few things, I will put you in charge of many things; enter into the joy of your master." The man who had been given two talents went forward showing the same results, and he was given an identical affirmation and invitation to move deeper into the joy of his master.

When the last slave reported in, however, his was a very different story. "Master, I knew that you were a harsh man, reaping where you did not sow, and gathering where you did not scatter seed; so I was afraid, and I went and hid your talent in the ground. Here you have what is yours."

At this, the master exploded. "You wicked and lazy slave! You knew that I reap where I did not sow, and gather where I did not scatter? Then you ought to have invested my money with the bankers, and on my return I would have received what was my own with interest. So take the talent from him," he commanded, "and give it to the one with the ten talents. For to all those who have, more will be given, and they will have an abundance; but from those who have nothing, even what they have will be taken away." He continued—and here I paraphrase in the idiom of our day—"Remove this worthless slave from me. He is totally out of sync with the dynamics of the universe."

What are we to make of these images? I think they confirm the fact that we are made in the image of a dynamic and creative God, and that we do taste God's kind of ecstasy when we imitate with our powers what we see God doing with his. The two slaves who were energetic and creative with their gifts modeled what God had in mind for creation from the very first. This universe about us is full of mystery indeed, but I think you can count on the fact that it is finally a fair and faithful place when you follow the example of the Holy One described so beautifully in Genesis. God freely used his power to delight himself and to bless all that he touched, and this is the pattern we are meant to follow as well.

This does not mean we will always at every moment get exactly what we think we want. There are many mysterious zigzags in the course of history, but at bottom there is also a faithfulness between what we sow and what we reap.

I remember some years ago reading a memorial oration that C. S. Lewis gave at King's College. Lewis told those highly privileged, well-placed young students that because of their education they would have great access to the corridors of power. He suggested that there were two ways they could approach their destiny. One way would be that of manipulation—to work first this angle and then that angle to finagle one's way quickly into as much power as possible. Those who took this shortcut to influence, however, would not likely develop the kind of skills that heavy responsibility ultimately demands.

The other route, Lewis contended, was to resolve to do good work; to take whatever was one's chosen discipline and learn how to do it thoroughly and well. This approach would be much slower, but in the end, other good workers would recognize the quality of their labors and grant them access to real power.

The second approach Lewis described is ultimately the only way into the true "inner ring." When we resolve to become good craftspersons in whatever field we choose, there will come a time when others will recognize our competence, and the influence of such effort will be a lasting one.[2] I do not believe this is a false or elusive promise. The point is, we live in a faithful and fruitful universe.

In Jesus' parable, the owner was not as interested in the quantity of what each was given as in their faithfulness to be creative and fruitful with their opportunities. It follows that God is not going to ask for the same results from each one of us because we have not all been given the same abilities or opportunities. What will be asked of us is, "What have you done with what you were given?"

There is a wonderful old parable that describes how, when one comes before the judgment seat of God, God will not ask, "Why weren't you Abraham?" or "Why weren't you Moses?" What God will want to know is, "Were you yourself? Did you do the best you could with what you had?" Remember, the whole purpose of existence is for us to experience God's kind of joy, and the secret here is to use our power and freedom in the same way God that God does—to delight himself and to bless all others.

Now we need to look at the shadow side of this parable: the third slave who was given only one talent and did not do anything with it. Here is a somber warning without doubt. There are two ways of being unfaithful. There is the "hot" way, which is to abuse our powers and use them destructively. This is the sin of commission. Then there is the "cold" way of being unfaithful, which is to do nothing at all and therefore neglect and abort one's potential.

Interestingly enough, in one of the apocryphal gospels there is a parable identical to this one except in one regard: the slave takes the one talent and goes out and wastes it on wine and women. When the master returns, the slave has nothing to show for his efforts. This illustrates the abusive use of power. The unfaithfulness we see in the incident described here, however, is that of a man who had done none of these things. His mistake was in doing nothing at all, simply burying what he had been given and neglecting it. This is the sin of omission, and it is just as serious, although its true effect is much slower in coming to light. The people who do nothing are never caught off base or red-handed, so it is very easy for them to be critical of the folks who are trying to do things but who visibly fail.

However, if you look carefully at the teachings of Jesus, he took the sin of under-utilizing what you could be just as seriously as the sin of over-utilizing in abuse. Sin is finally a matter of trying to be either more or less than we ought to be, and either way we "fall short of the glory of God," as Paul put it in Romans 3:23. Because of the seriousness of this issue, let us look more closely at what may have caused this tragic missing of the mark. What went wrong here? Why was the divine pattern of things disrupted? The most obvious explanation is simple inertia: the slave did not want to put forth the effort to undertake a more creative route. Burying his talent in the ground was the lazy way of handling his responsibility.

Author M. Scott Peck goes so far as to say that inertia may be the essence of original sin. He points to the third chapter of Genesis, where the serpent made certain damaging accusations against God. Peck makes the point that if the first man and woman had proceeded to research the matter energetically—that is, if they had gone to God and said, "Here is what the serpent said about you. Is it true?"—they could have easily discovered that they were being told a pack of lies. However, that is precisely what they did not do. They lazily accepted without investigation what the serpent had implied and proceeded to act upon it.[3]

A second possibility for his failure, however, may have been jealousy and envy. The slave with one talent was bound to have noticed what had been entrusted to his other colleagues; he may have focused more energy on the hands they had been dealt than on the possibilities that were his to exercise. The sidelong glance is a sure way to lose our focus and get deflected from our own mission. Jesus reminded Simon Peter of that very risk right before his ascension. The two had become reconciled by the Sea of Galilee. Jesus totally forgave Peter and set him once again to the task of feeding his sheep. It was a moment of genuine restoration, but then seeing John, Peter began to inquire about his destiny. Jesus retorted bluntly, "That is none of your business, Peter. You have your commission to perform. Focus on that and not idle speculation!" (John 21:22) Perhaps the third slave lost sight of his responsibility when his focus was deflected by noticing what the others had been given.

A third possibility may have been that the smallness of his talent led him to conclude that what he did with it did not matter. If I believe anything at all, it is this: in God's universe, there is nothing that is insignificant. The great things were first of all little things that were lifted up to God in reverence and gratitude, and then used to the fullest. It is a mistake to confuse size with value.

Nashville music publisher Bob Benson recognized this fact quite clearly. He tells about his son being given a bit part in an elementary school play. The lad had hoped for better things, but he was relegated to having only two lines close to the end of the whole production. The performance took place on a hot May evening, and this is what Benson wrote in his journal that night: "Mike was not a star, by any means, but he waited faithfully, and when his moment came, he was ready. He said his lines, and he said them well—not too soon, not too late, not too loud, not too soft, but just right." Then Benson went on to reflect:

I am just a bit player too, not a star in any sense of the word, but God gave me a line or so in the pageant of life, and when the curtain falls and the drama ends and the stage is vacant at last, I do not ask for the critic's rave or fame in any amount. My only hope is this—that I can hear from afar the voice of God saying, "He said his lines and he said them well—not too soon, not too late, not too loud, not too soft. He said his lines, and he said them well!"[4]

There is nothing insignificant that comes from the hand of God. I cannot help but wonder, however, if that one-talent man failed to realize the incredible significance of the tiny things that were given to him.

I suppose that any of these factors could account for his missing the mark, but the text itself suggests that the real problem was one of mistrust. The slave acknowledged as much when he said to the owner, "I knew that you were a harsh man." He went on to accuse him of being dishonest, and then claimed it was his own fear that led him to bury the talent. "Who knows what someone like you would have done to me if I had lost it?" he thought to himself. Then he returned it saying, "Here you have what is yours."

Once again, we encounter that greatest of all dehumanizers—the reality of fear. Nothing distorts our humanity quite as much as the sense that there is not enough and therefore one has to fight or flee. Of course, more than anything else, this distortion is what Jesus came to cast out. The serpent put the whole human race off track by casting false aspersions on God's character. He projected onto God

48

what this slave projected onto his master—that God was hard, cruel, dishonest, and untrustworthy. It was to undo this misrepresentation that Jesus entered into history.

In a study group, I heard author John Killinger claim that "Jesus was God's answer to the problem of a bad reputation." Killinger believes that reconciliation finally occurs when we let Jesus "show us the Father" and disprove forever the serpent's distortion. What this slave did out of fear is an analogy for what we humans do when we picture God fearfully instead of lovingly. We not only violate our own natures by becoming either more or less than we are, but we also unmake the whole creation that God has so carefully crafted. This is why Jesus takes the actions of this fearful slave so seriously. The fate of being cast into utter darkness is not meant to describe what God wants at all, but rather how important it is that we see God's true nature and then begin to live our lives accordingly. "It is not the will of your Father in heaven that one of these little ones should be lost," Jesus said (Matthew 18:14). To warn against such a fate and to show us the way of salvation is why this parable was told.

Remember, it is not too late for anyone. We all can see what Jesus came into the world to show—the nurturing nature of God, so much like that of a firm but compassionate parent—and then begin to act out of love, not fear.

Well, what are we waiting for?

Chapter Four

THE GREAT BANQUET

One of the dinner guests, on hearing this, said to him, "Blessed is anyone who will eat bread in the kingdom of God!" Then Jesus said to him, "Someone gave a great dinner and invited many. At the time for the dinner he sent his slave to say to those who had been invited, 'Come; for everything is ready now.' But they all alike began to make excuses. The first said to him, 'I have bought a piece of land, and I must go out and see it; please accept my regrets.' Another said, 'I have bought five yoke of oxen, and I am going to try them out; please accept my regrets.' Another said, 'I have just been married, and therefore I cannot come.' So the slave returned and reported this to his master. Then the owner of the house became angry and said to his slave, 'Go out at once into the streets and lanes of the town and bring in the poor, the crippled, the blind, and the lame.' And the slave said, 'Sir, what you ordered has been done, and there is still room.'

*Then the master said to the slave, 'Go out into the
roads and lanes, and compel people to come in, so
that my house may be filled. For I tell you, none of
those who were invited will taste my dinner.'"*

LUKE 14:15-24

There are several motifs that occur again and
again in Holy Scripture, and one of them is central to this particular story that Jesus told. It revolves
around the generous hospitality of a host giving a
party, and the response of those invited to such graciousness. This is actually the framework that the
Bible sets around the whole drama of history. So let
us look carefully at the words of this parable and
allow them to permeate our imaginations and our
very lives.

I can think of no better image for the biblical
understanding of God than that of a host or a gracious party-giver. Paul Tillich claims he was launched
on his philosophic quest as a fourteen-year-old when
someone posed the question, "Why something and
not nothing?" In other words, why does anything
exist, or "stand out of nothingness" as the word literally means? If you allow Holy Scripture to be your
resource here, the answer reverberates back: God is
the link between nothingness and being—and not
just any God, but a generous one who wants to take
what he is and has and share this with others.

Do you see, then, why Jesus' metaphor of a host
giving a party is so apt? No image better gathers up
the things that are revealed in Holy Scripture about
God than this one. Here are generosity, abundance,
joyfulness, and exuberance all bound up together.
The very best kind of parties are not given out of
necessity or obligation. Truth be told, that is the reason behind many of them, but occasionally people

throw a bash for no other reason save that they love a good time and want to share with their friends. There is something authentically healthy about those things that come out of the "want to" side of our personality. These realities are very different from what comes out of the "have to" side of things. The impulse to share what is good and not keep it all to ourselves is also a sign of personal maturity.

I lived out much of my young adulthood in Louisville, Kentucky, having gone to school there and then returning to serve a parish for eleven years. About halfway into that experience, a friend said to me, "I have just discovered a country inn about thirty miles south of here near Brandenburg. It used to be an old stagecoach stop. Somebody has gone in, reclaimed the old building, and opened a restaurant called Doe Run Inn. I'd love to take you there someday. It's a secret that is too good to keep."

Not long after that, we did go. It was a nice trip out of the city and into the tranquil countryside. The inn was located in a beautiful valley with lots of shade trees. There was a stream running right beside it where you could still see the old mill wheel, and a screened porch where you could sit and hear the running water. The food was excellent, and the atmosphere relaxing. It turned out to be a perfect way to spend an evening.

You can anticipate my response to that experience. Hardly a week went by before I found myself doing exactly what my friend had done: I was telling someone else about Doe Run Inn and arranging to take them there. Over the next few years, I took sixty or seventy people to that lovely old place, and the people I took began to introduce it to others. My point is, there is something about goodness that makes you want to share it.

This is precisely how the Bible accounts for everything coming to be. The transcendent Holy One is also the Generous One. One way of describing creation, then, is to see it as the party God has chosen to throw so that we can get in on some of his bounty and begin to know the joy of being party-givers ourselves.

Thus, our parable begins on a familiar note. A host who had a house and food and all kinds of abundance wanted to share this with others, but then things took an unexpected turn. The generosity of the party-giver was not met by gratitude or a positive willingness to respond. Amazingly, those who had received engraved invitations began to snub the host. When he sent his car around to pick them up, so to speak, they began to make all kinds of excuses and wound up refusing to attend at all.

Here is yet another parallel to the creation story, for we do not get past the third chapter of Genesis before it becomes clear that what God wanted for creation and what followed are not the same thing at all. Early on in the biblical story, the shadow of evil falls straight across the bright intention of the Creator. "Where did this evil come from," one has to wonder, and "Why was it allowed to exist in the first place?"

To put the issue quite bluntly, if God is all-powerful and all-good, as the Bible seems to imply, why is there so much in God's creation that is painful and destructive? Could not such a Being have structured things somehow to prevent all that is so clearly at odds with the reality of joy from existing at all? This is the hardest question that believing people have to face, just as the reality of good is the hardest issue for those who have no faith and claim to be atheists. The latter are called on to account for the presence of so much beauty and purpose on the premise that there is no God, while the believer's dilemma centers on the presence of evil.

No issue has inspired more debate across the centuries than this one. For example, a popular treatment of the subject is Harold Kushner's book, *When Bad Things Happen To Good People*. Kushner takes the approach that many have adopted, arguing that we have to alter the ancient concept of God to account for evil. He believes that of the three assertions—God is all-powerful, God is all-good, and evil exists—only two can be embraced simultaneously, not all three. This means we can say that evil is real and God is all-powerful, but then God cannot be all-good, or else God would surely eliminate evil. If God could put an end to evil and does not, this casts a shadow on God's goodness. Or we could say that if God is all-good and evil exists, there must be a deficiency in God's power. If God really wants to eliminate evil but cannot, then we can no longer support the claim that God is omnipotent.[1]

A third alternative, one the Christian Scientists accept, is that evil does not really exist, but is only an illusion. This leaves the two other affirmations about God intact. But in a world that has witnessed the Holocaust, it is hard to be realistic and still believe that all this violence and evil is merely in our minds and imagination.

Kushner himself opts for the first combination. He concludes that the problem lies in God's power—that God, like us, is up against what he calls a "randomness" in the world that even God cannot master.[2] A great many serious thinkers have resolved the dilemma in this way: they conclude that evil exists because God is lacking in power. In Woody Allen's words, "I am not saying there is no God. I am

simply saying that if One does exist, he is an under-
achiever!"

I do not claim that I can resolve the mystery of
evil better than all these other thinkers. But through
my own intellectual struggles, I have come to a different conclusion than those I have just described.
Let us go back for a moment and recall God's reason
for creating in the first place. I have been contending
all through this book that God's only intention in
creating was to share his own special kind of joy. The
wonder of God's aliveness was regarded as too good
to hold back. God wanted others to participate in the
ecstasy he was experiencing in being who he was.
There was no emptiness in God that needed to be
filled. There was rather a bottomless fullness God
wanted to share. This, then, is the final intention,
and it raises the question, "What would God have to
do to make this desire a reality?"

When we break down this question, we can discern three essential ingredients that enable us to participate in God's kind of joy. Human creatures have
to be given a measure of power—the ability to make
things happen. They also need to possess a measure
of freedom. The divine Being is not some mechani-
cal robot, but a living Spirit who freely chooses to
create, and then freely takes delight in what has
been created. The third ingredient is a spirit of wisdom that knows how to use power in ways that
bring delight to God's self and blessing to all who
are affected by these actions. To act is to make a difference, to alter the situation into which power is
asserted. The secret of God's unique quality of spirit is that the difference God made was not just
pleasing to God or to others, but pleasing to both
simultaneously.

These three ingredients, it seems to me, assure that God's joy can be shared by all of us. Not even an omnipotent God could have created the possibility for joy in any other way, which underlines the fact that the risk of failure was inherent in the goal God wanted to achieve. God could have withheld either power or freedom, and thus evil could never have been—but then the reality of joy would have been impossible as well.

This really is the best of all possible worlds, it seems to me, given what God wanted to accomplish. Evil did not come into existence because there is some flaw in God's power or goodness. Its presence roots back to the freedom that had to be given in order for joy to be possible—and this would not have been true freedom if it could not have been used negatively as well as positively.

If you take the biblical stories seriously, the root of evil lies in the spirit possessed by the first human beings. In the Genesis account, the serpent challenged the idea that God was totally good. "He is not one who always acts to bless those he touches," the serpent inferred. "He is at heart a tyrant, an exploiter, one who is holding you down in order to build himself up."

In other words, the serpent accused God of thinking only of his own delight rather than of those affected by his actions—and he encouraged Adam, Eve, and all humankind to do the same thing. Whenever we pull asunder what seems to be joined together in God—personal delight and the will to bless—some form of evil results. The serpent's allegations against God prompted the humans to forget all about blessing others, and in panic to look out for themselves alone. Consequently, they stopped using their power to follow God's example, and the result was the unmaking of God's creation. The Holy One started with nothing and moved through chaos to order and beauty. Once God's way of acting was rejected, and only "what is good for number one" began to shape behavior, order and beauty were turned back into chaos and finally into nothingness itself.

Why did this happen? I repeat, it is not because there is a flaw in the design. If God's kind of joy is to be realized, there has to be power and freedom and a certain kind of spirit. It was when that spirit became distorted that the whole thing began to unravel.

"Evil" really is "live" spelled backwards, and it grows out of the very possibilities that had to exist for joy to be. Thus, instead of blaming God for evil and saying God is lacking in either power or good-ness, I think we need to realize that it is we humans who have taken what God gave us and misused it. The problem is not that God has insufficient power, but rather that no amount of power could create the reality of joy coercively. What God is and wants for us is finally something highly personal. When we enter that realm, sheer brute force can only go so far.

I remember well when my son was about to have his sixth birthday. We wanted this to be a special milestone for him, so we bought the presents we thought he most wanted and invited his best friends to a great celebration. For some reason, however, the lad had gotten up on the wrong side of the bed that morning, and nothing that whole day turned out to please him. He hated our presents and sulked through the whole party. Although I forced him physically to be present, there was no power in the world that could make him enjoy the occasion. Joy is finally something a human being has to experience willingly—and not even an all-good, all-powerful God can force that reality on another free spirit.

Returning to our parable, then, the host did all he could to set the stage for an experience of joy. What he did not have the power to do was to coerce his guests to come or to enjoy what was there once they arrived; they were the only ones who could complete this particular process. Why did they choose not to? Why do human beings who were made for joy in the first place choose to turn away in misery? There is no logical explanation for such self-destructive behavior. The Bible speaks of "the mystery of iniquity." That is what evil is ultimately—a deep and dark mystery. Why it happens, no one can finally say. That it happens and that we ourselves participate in it, who can deny?

So what took place in the parable when the desire of the party-giver was finally thwarted? His first reaction was one of anger. Can you blame him? People are very uncomfortable with the image of "the wrath of God," for they say it does not square with a God of love and mercy and joyfulness. However, think again about the true nature of love. The opposite of this reality is not anger but indifference. We never get angry about something that is unimportant to us. There is always an element of concern involved in an outburst of anger because something that truly matters has been violated. For the host to have shown no feeling at being rejected would have revealed that he did not care about the guests in the first place, and indifference would be inconsistent with the nature of authentic love.

The wrath of God, then, does not consist of the Almighty having an immature temper tantrum because he cannot have his way. It grows out of deep frustration and sadness when the blessings God wants to give are being thwarted or even ignored. The wrath of God is truly an aspect of the love of God, a sign of how deeply the holy One cares and wants to bless.

The host's second response, however, was not to give up on the idea of a party altogether, but to widen the invitation list. He sent out his servants to get the poor, the lame, the people who had massive physical problems. When these efforts did not fill up the hall, he sent out into countryside, into "the roads and lanes," and invited the most socially unsophisticated of all the people in the community, those who would never have dreamed of being in the manor house.

This facet of the story, of course, has an historical dimension to it, similar to Jesus' story about the petulant children. Jesus was defending himself and explaining why he had done what he did in his ministry. He had been roundly criticized because he ate with sinners. It had offended the religious establishment that he had reached out so deliberately to social outcasts. Jesus was constantly being judged for the kind of company he kept, and one of the things that he was doing here was holding up a mirror so those who criticized him could see themselves.

The Jewish people were the very first ones who had been invited by God to come and enjoy the divine bounty. The Holy One said to Abraham, "I want to bless you and through you all the families of the earth." One of the objectives in giving the party was God's desire that the party-goers would also get into the spirit of it. Had that happened, God's desire and joy would have spread out universally.

Of course, some Jews did not so respond, but that did not quench the sharing impulses of God anymore than the establishment's rejection of Jesus discouraged him. God's turning to the tax collectors and sinners is of one piece with God's tenacious mercy. This story simply gives powerful expression to the deepest dimension of the gospel. While there is nothing we can do to make God love us any more than God already does, neither is there anything we can do to make God stop loving us. There is both a stubbornness and an ingenuity in God's way of loving. God does not take away our freedom or shield us from the consequences of our evil, but often through those very traumas God brings us to a new awareness.

In reading the parable of the prodigal son (Luke 15:11-32), some people are shocked that the father would give the younger son his share of the inheritance when the young man's spirit was so rebellious and his immaturity so great. Wasn't it folly to hand over matches to one who knew so little about fire? However, this is precisely how God's wisdom works in relation to our freedom. God allows us to learn for ourselves through pain what we refuse to be taught from those wiser than we are, and in the prodigal's case, it worked! In the far country, he was dumb enough to lose all that his father had been smart enough to make and to save. He finally wound up in the lowest place a Jewish boy could possibly go—having to feed pigs, of all things! He collided head-on with all his faulty notions of himself, the world, and his father. There, in the pit of failure, Jesus said, "He came to himself"—a medical term meaning to wake up from a coma. This moment marked the turning point in the son's process of maturing.

This parable should be very reassuring to the parents of those teenagers who seemingly refuse to listen to anything they are being taught. Even in the midst of headlong rebellion and self-destructive behavior, God is not absent or without resources to bless. Self-imposed pain is ofttimes a great teacher, which explains why neither God nor Jesus had abandoned hope for the lowliest of the outcasts. These folk were often the most ripe for coming to themselves precisely because of what their mistakes had taught them.

Remember, God is far more interested in our future than in our past, and more concerned about what we have learned from our mistakes than the fact that we have made them. Notice carefully that when the prodigal does venture back home, he encounters nothing but gladness and acceptance from his father. His father does not say a word about the inheritance the prodigal had lost. The important thing is what he has learned, not what it has cost.

Here is a wonderful reminder that it is never too late to turn back to the merciful Father. Once a child, always a child. We did not create our relationship with God by what we did; therefore, we cannot forfeit or destroy that relationship by what we do or fail to do. The bond between us is God's gift to us. Letting our sin teach us what we need to learn is part of the way that God's mercy works. My hunch is that the people who were invited last were not only the most ready but the most astonished of all. They realized they had wasted their substance and been arrogant and unwise. Out there in the darkness, they might have assumed that their badness was bigger than anything else, that they had forfeited forever the chance to sit at the table and get a glimpse of the party-giver's face. The wonder of what the prodigal discovered was the wonder that broke over these individuals as well: they were still included in spite of all they had done! Lo and behold, God's goodness was bigger than their badness, and those who knew best how little they deserved it appreciated it the most.

Yet we must not miss the note of warning that is inherent in this story. Mark it down: with all his heart, God wants us to come to his party of joy, but at the same time it is possible to miss out on the party altogether. The reason is not because creation is flawed, but that you and I are ultimately free. We are the only ones who can sense that God's spirit of delighting and blessing is the essence of reality, the only ones who can decide to embrace that spirit and begin to embody it.

You see, we can miss the party by being arrogant and destructive in the way we use our power, or we can miss it by being so caught up in everyday routine that we confuse the good for the best and never really get around to being what we could be.

What I am trying to suggest is that there are ways to miss the party that are not blatantly evil. If we take a look at the three excuses that were made in the parable, two of them had to do with work and the other had to do with family. These people confused the good for the best, and settled for living at a level far below the joy God wanted for them.

The final warning is that we can miss the place that has been prepared for us from the foundations of the earth by absolutely defying God's design of creation and living in total opposition to God's way of love, or we can drift into such mediocrity that the high purpose of God is lost by neglect. We can miss the kingdom by being so caught up in our own routines that we fail by default.

I want to close this chapter by quoting a homily written by a Lutheran minister. The first time I heard it, I was startled by the way it immediately became a parable for me, enabling me to see as in a mirror. My hope is that this homily will do its redemptive work in you as well:

Herman closed the front door gently, took off his coat, and hung it in the closet. He unzipped his overshoes, first one and then the other, slid them off, and bent down to put them in the closet. There a wild jumble of boots and rubbers confronted him. Muttering under his breath, he began to sort them out and arrange them two by two. Then he carefully placed his own side by side in the last square inch of space and tried to close the door. It would not close. A parka that had been jammed in hurriedly was blocking the door. Herman methodically rearranged the coats and jackets and sweaters. Then he closed the door gently.

For one flashing second he thought, "Why didn't I just slam that door? Why didn't I just throw my overshoes in on top of the heap like everybody else does?" But it was only a momentary spasm. "One just does not do things that way," he said to himself.

The house was strangely quiet. The cat meowed plaintively and rubbed against his leg. He stooped over and patted her.

"Hello, Mrs. Beasley."

Funny name for a cat, but Tammy had insisted on calling her Mrs. Beasley after she'd seen a television doll commercial. A ridiculous name for a cat really.

"I wanted to call her Whiskers or Tabby, but Tammy insisted on Mrs. Beasley," Herman recalled, smiling to himself. "Mrs. Beasley."

The cat followed him to the refrigerator. He poured some milk into her dish and opened a new can of cat food.

"Where is everybody?" he asked the cat as he spooned out food into her dish. Then Herman closed the refrigerator door gently.

"Last minute shopping, I guess."

He mused about it as he went upstairs to take off his clothes.

"Lorraine is always shopping at the last minute. Well, not always, but a good bit of the time. Probably wieners and beans for dinner tonight."

He was mildly irritated. The bedroom was a shambles. Lorraine's slacks and blouse were thrown on the bed. The closet doors were flung open. A dress hung askew on a crooked hanger. Her shoes had obviously been quickly rummaged through. He sighed and opened the closet door gently. He hung his suit away, then carried his shirt to the clothes hamper in the bathroom. He had to push Tammy's sneakers off the mat as he hung up her towel. He scooped up her play clothes and crammed them together with his shirt into the hamper.

"Life would be so much easier if people would just take a little time to be more tidy. It would make my job easier too," he thought as he ran water into the sink.

He had to plan his day. This was Herman's way—the only way he could manage to retain any semblance of sanity. Then inevitably somebody came along and disrupted his plans. Suddenly a great weariness came over him. As he leaned on his hands in the water, random thoughts begin to flicker through his mind like fragments of a ragged film running through a broken projector. Would the company expand or relocate? Maybe we will have to move. Jennings would sure like my job—he is a manipulator. The house needs painting. The living room rug is pretty worn. Has the washing machine been repaired? Wonder how much it was? Tammy's tooth is loose; maybe it will drop out. Jennings has just built a new house. His payments must be very steep—no wonder he wants my job. At least Lorraine sews her own clothes; that is a help. We have got to throw a party soon—there are lots of invitations to pay back. Oh, the pledge card from the church, it has just come. Got to get the car winterized; should have it sanded and painted if I am going to drive it another year. I wonder if we will get any tax breaks this year? Didn't get anything done today like I planned. That dumb Jennings—he messed up my whole afternoon—had to drop everything and go to a special session to consider his harebrained plans. He seems to think he is the only idea man in the company. How do they expect me to get my work done with all these interruptions?

He dressed and closed his closet door gently. He picked up Lorraine's slacks and blouse and hung them away. "Poor girl! I know she gets fed up with her daily routines. Breakfast, cleaning, getting Tammy off to kindergarten, cooking, washing, ironing. I know she would like to get out. At least I see grown people every day. This house must be like a prison to her." He closed her closet door gently and went downstairs. Mrs. Beasley rubbed his leg and he picked her up.

"Six o'clock—wherever could they be?"

He started to sort through the mail, and it was then that he saw the note.

"Herman, we waited until almost five for you and then just had to leave. Please get a cab and join us. You missed Tammy's birthday party last year. Try not to miss it again this year. Lorraine!"

Tammy's birthday party. At a restaurant that caters such things. They had planned it together. He had been a little reluctant at first, but okay, the sixth birthday is a milestone, and he could see Tammy that very morning saying, "Daddy, you'll be there, won't you?" and he had given her a big hug.

He looked at the clock, and it said 6:15. Somewhere in his soul, Herman heard a door slam shut. The kingdom of heaven, so it is said, is like the time a man received an invitation—even conscientious Hermans can miss the party because they mistake the good for the best.[3]

We have all been invited, brothers and sisters. Please do not let anything cause you to overlook that or forget it—please!

Chapter Five

THE PETULANT CHILDREN

To what then will I compare the people of this generation, and what are they like? They are like children sitting in the marketplace and calling to one another,
"We played the flute for you,
and you did not dance;
we wailed, and you did not weep."
For John the Baptist has come eating no bread and drinking no wine, and you say, "He has a demon"; the Son of Man has come eating and drinking, and you say, "Look, a glutton and a drunkard, a friend of tax collectors and sinners!" Nevertheless, wisdom is vindicated by all her children.

Luke 7:31-35

The setting of this story is a typical Palestinian village in the days of Jesus, an open square with children playing noisily in every direction. To this day, children of that region have the run of the whole town. As there was very little privacy or comfort in individual homes, public spaces became the setting where everyone spent most of their waking hours.

Writer Kenneth Bailey served for many years as a missionary in Lebanon. This exposure gives him unusual insight into the details of so many of the parables. For example, in commenting on the parable of the prodigal son, Bailey makes much of the fact that although the younger son was "still far off," his old father saw him and ran to "put his arms around him and kissed him" (Luke 15:20). Bailey claims that the father did this to protect the returning son from the children of the village who ran in packs and would have been quick to taunt and badger. They would have wanted to know why he was dressed so shabbily and what happened to all the arrogant boasts he had made as he had left.

These same children, however, are now the primary focus in this story. Every parent or teacher will quickly recognize the dynamics Jesus is describing here. In any gathering of children, there are usually two distinct groups—"the proposers" and "the reactors." To the question "What shall we do?" there are always the idea persons who come up with specific suggestions. In this parable, the first proposal was "Let's play wedding. Let's dress up in our parents' clothes and act like we are getting married. Then, after the ceremony, we can have a feast and dance and imitate all the joyful things we have seen our parents doing."

In that sparse and hard culture, weddings were the happiest of all occasions. For a blessed interval, the peasants could lay down their tools and let themselves go in the feasting and merrymaking. If you have seen the musical *Fiddler on the Roof,* you may remember the incredible exuberance that characterized the wedding of Tevye's first daughter. So the proposers said, "Let's play wedding and imitate the joy of the adults," but the reactors said, "We don't want to play wedding. We don't feel like it. We don't want to do happy things right now. We are not in the mood for it." The proposers, however, prove to be quite adaptable and flexible. Today we might classify them as codependents: folk who are more tuned in to what others want than to what they want or need for themselves. One wag has said, "When a codependent is drowning, another person's life flashes before his eyes." They may not know what *they* feel, but they are very aware of what *others* feel and want. Thus, when the reactors say, "We don't feel like playing wedding," the proposers say, "Okay, so you are feeling bad. Let's go with where *you* are. Let's play funeral. We'll imagine that someone has died. We have seen how the big people wail and scream and dress in black. If you are feeling as bad as you say you are, then let's play funeral and act like the worst has happened."

If a wedding was the high point of joy in the Palestinian culture, the funeral experience was located at the opposite end of the spectrum: it was a season of great heaviness and mourning. Here you have the two extremes in human experience. But lo and behold, the same children who do not want to play wedding reply testily, "No, we don't want to play funeral either. That is not appealing to us." At this point, the proposers became frustrated and asked,

"What is it with you people? We piped, and you did not want to dance. We wailed, and you did not want to weep. For God's sake, what *do* you want to do?"

What Jesus is mirroring here is one of the deepest problems in all human life: the presence of a spirit of chronic dissatisfaction no matter what a person's circumstances may be. The transactional analysis people describe a certain behavior as a game called "Yes, But," in which individuals asking for help promptly reject out of hand whatever is proposed. Here, in the image of hordes of petulant children, Jesus raises up an issue of towering significance for us all, one with both a historical and a personal dimension.

First of all, Jesus uses this story to describe where he was in the unfolding of his own career. You may remember that Jesus experienced resounding success when he first began his ministry. People flocked to him by the hundreds. But then, as time went on, the kind of chronic dissatisfaction that characterized these children began to surface: criticism of who he was and how he lived his life began to mount. At this stage, he told the parable of the sower and the various kinds of soils—how some seed fell on rocks or on shallow soil or among thorns (Luke 8:4-8). It was his way of coming to terms with failure and rejection. He was learning that three out of every four things he wanted to do would not be actualized because of factors beyond his control.

This little parable reflects the same sort of realism on Jesus' part. He describes in pictorial language what was happening right before his eyes. You see, in that very era of history God had launched a powerful initiative to bring redemption to the world. The two chief figures in this movement were actually cousins, John the Baptist and Jesus. In many ways, these two were quite different in terms of how they went about their work.

They illustrate the two forms of change-strategies that have been tried across the centuries to take bad situations and make them better. One is called "the revolutionary approach." Here you attack a problem from the outside. You dramatize the difficulty by having someone who is not immersed in it come and say clearly, "Here is what is wrong and here is what you have to do if you are going to change and survive." The folk who do this are called "radicals," and they usually promise all kinds of doom if something is not done.

Back in the 1960s, such radicals were prominent in our culture. In Jesus' day, John the Baptist was the embodiment of this approach to personal and social change. He stands in the tradition of the Old Testament prophets. His insights were clear, and he had abundant courage. John was willing to stand up to anyone. He stated quite forthrightly that if things did not change soon, terrible consequences were sure to follow.

John was the consummate outsider. He dressed in sparse, desert fashion, and would not eat anything but locusts and wild honey. He did not touch any kind of strong drink and was very confrontational in the way he related to the culture. What happens to most revolutionary prophets happened to John the Baptist. At first, he created quite a stir, but he so frightened people by his dire predictions that they began to regard him as crazy or totally out of touch with reality. He was finally arrested by the authorities and beheaded down on the shores of the Dead Sea.

On the other hand, Jesus came as a very different sort of change-agent. He was more evolutionary than revolutionary. He chose initially to identify with people and connect with their concerns rather than to set himself over against them. His approach was to breathe new life on slumbering embers, to take the good that was already there and find a way to make it grow—a very different approach than that of the radical who comes in with fire in the eyes and says, "Unless you change, terrible things are going to happen to you." This kind of change-agent starts by coming close with tears in his eyes, not fire. He says "we" instead of "you" in describing the problems. He dares to get down where his own hands become dirty, where he suffers what other people are suffering, and from that perspective he seeks to call forth the best and to cast out the worst.

This is the way that Jesus went about the redemptive task. First of all, he identified himself with the people whom he was trying to save. He became what the people were so that they might become what he was. He ate what they ate, drank what they drank, and dressed like they dressed. He loved a good party. One of the first times we see him in John's gospel, he is present at a wedding feast. He even bails out the embarrassed host by turning some water into wine. He was the joyous life of every party he ever attended and was known to all for his convivial spirit.

So what did the people of that day say of this Jesus who chose to work from within rather than from without? Truth be told, they rejected him with the same kind of chronic negativism that the petulant children displayed. When he began his mission, the common people heard him gladly. He proceeded to love each one he ever met as if there were no one else in all the world to love, and he loved all as he loved each. He excluded no one from the circle of his affection and came to be known as "the Bridegroom of the World." Jesus identified with the least and the last and the worst, and what happened? The very same people who had rejected John the Baptist for being too negative and too austere rejected Jesus for being too loving and too lax! The very people who had said, "John is crazy in his idealism," then said of Jesus, "He is no better than all the rest. Why, he is a friend of sinners. I saw him eating the other day at table with some tax collectors. He is a drunkard and a glutton. There is no difference between him and the worst people in society."

In the experience of those who originally heard these words, two very different approaches to redeeming the world had been tried, and the people of that era wound up rejecting both of them! Therefore, the little story about the petulant children was first of all a description of that moment in history, and how the best that God had to offer was not enough because of the negative mind-set of the very people Jesus came to save.

Although this parable does say a great deal about the conditions of that particular era in history, there is also another critical dimension. How does the parable apply to us and our attitudes, and how do we handle the ways God is trying to save us? It would be easy to point accusing fingers and say, "Can you imagine people having the benefit of somebody as wise as John the Baptist and not learning from him? Can you imagine people experiencing the love of Jesus and not letting that nurture them back to wholeness? Isn't it incredible how the people of that day were so out of it?"

However, such an approach would miss the main point of this parable. A chronic condition of dissatisfaction—not really liking anything—is a basic problem with many of us. This is the very depth of evil in the human condition that Jesus came to confront, the wound that Jesus most wants to touch and to heal. In fact, I see this spirit of chronic dissatisfaction as the essence of sin and the polar opposite of what Holy Scripture says to us about the nature of God.

I have referred time and time again to the story in Genesis of how the One who is the wellspring of life decided to share that life with others. God felt his aliveness was something too good to keep to himself. God wanted others to taste his form of ecstasy, which consisted of freely choosing to create, effectively carrying through on that resolve, and finally looking with delight on what he had done. The one thing you do not find anywhere in Genesis is a note of dissatisfaction. God did not create out of some unhappy need in himself that God was trying selfishly to fill, nor was he displeased with the outcome. God's evaluation of the whole process is summed up in that exuberant refrain: "It is good! It is good! It is very, very good!"

Now obviously, something had occurred between that beginning moment of creation and the moment Jesus describes in the village square as he tells this parable. From whence did this utterly different attitude toward reality come? The Bible suggests that it is the bitter fruit of evil entering our human experience. The opposite of what God had intended is precisely what these petulant children represent.

If we were to put this problem in contemporary psychological terms, we would call it *neurotic negativism*. Karen Horney is widely recognized as one of the pioneer researchers in this area. She makes a simple distinction between two terms that are often confused: *psychotic* and *neurotic*. A psychotic person, she affirms, is one who says, "Two plus two is five"; that is, he or she is out of touch with reality altogether. A neurotic individual, however, is one who says, "Two plus two is four, but I do not like it!" In other words, such people are in touch with reality, but it does not please them at all. They are realists, all right, but disgruntled and unhappy ones.[1]

There is a telling story about an English family who went on a picnic one day by the side of a beautiful lake. At one point their three-year-old son accidentally fell into the water, and none of the adults in the family knew how to swim. Here was the child, bobbing up and down in the water and screaming for help, and here was the family jumping up and down on the bank in near hysteria. A man who happened to be passing by quickly sized up the situation, and at great risk to his own safety, dove into the lake and rescued the boy before he sank for the final time. He climbed out on the bank with the child, who was badly frightened but basically all right, only to hear the mother ask testily, "Where is Johnny's cap?"

Let me suggest that this is classic neurotic behavior—the decision not to be satisfied no matter what the circumstances. We need to get in touch with the degree to which this way of seeing life is buried deeply in our own psyches. Indeed, this condition can be traced all the way back to what Genesis says happened to the whole race: our earliest forebears bought into the serpent's lie about the nature of God.

On a more personal level, however, this way of seeing life goes back to our perception of our own beginnings, according to Karen Horney. She traces the roots of neuroticism to what she calls "basic anxiety about one's self." And where does that anxiety come from? Horney suggests that if our very creation at birth is regarded as something negative—that is, if one is dissatisfied with the body one has been given, the mind one has, the family system into which one was born, or the era of history in which one finds oneself—then it follows rather consistently that everything after birth will appear negative as well. This perception is the poison spring from which all neurotic feelings and behaviors flow.[2]

I am reminded of a continuum I saw years ago during the era when transactional analysis was so popular in our culture. The leader of a seminar I was attending drew a long diagram on the blackboard that contained a center and then five positions in either direction. He labeled one side +1, +2, +3, +4, +5, and wrote the same numerals in a negative sequence in the other direction. These positions were defined this way: +1 stood for "I'm OK"; +2, "You're OK"; +3, "We're OK"; +4, "They're OK"; and +5, "It's OK." The negative sequence had the same pattern, only it read "I'm not OK," "You're not OK," "We're not OK," "They're not OK," and "It's not OK." The leader then designated the center point as the event of birth, and said that the way one chose to image that particular event set the tone for how one perceived everything else in life.

If I regard the first thing that God ever did to me as something good, then all the individuals and in-groups and out-groups and the whole of reality will come to be regarded in a positive light as well. But if I choose to look on my birth event as something negative, the shadow of that initial displeasure will eventually swallow up everything else, and all that I subsequently encounter will be evaluated negatively.

Years ago in seminary, a professor said that Jesus' words about "loving our neighbors as ourselves" were a psychological principle as well as an ethical challenge. I will never forget his saying forcefully, "You will love your neighbors as you love yourself. The way you choose to perceive the first person you encounter in history—namely, yourself—will lay down the tracks, so to speak, for all the other relationships that follow."

This assertion ties in exactly with Karen Horney's contention, for what is "basic anxiety about one's self" but the decision to regard negatively the beginning point of our life? You see, if our original forebears had trusted the goodness of their own creation and been able to say from the start, "I really am OK as I came from the hand of God," then the serpent's suggestion that they become like gods would have never taken root. They could have replied: "We don't want to be gods. Being human is good enough in itself." A basic anxiety about their self-worth opened the door to the suspicion that they were in fact "not OK," and that is how the whole human race got turned in the wrong direction.

Some time ago I came across this quotation from a book entitled *Concepts of Personality* that sums up the effects of the fall quite graphically:

> A sense of security is only possible if one is sure of his place, sure of his ability to cope with whatever may come, and sure of his worth and value. Anyone who believes he must energetically seek his place will never find it. He does not know that by his mere presence he already does belong and has a place. If one has to be more than he is in order to be somebody, he will never be anybody. If one does not realize that he is good enough as he is, he will never have any reason to assume he is good enough, regardless of how much money, power, or superiority he may amass. Few people believe they are good enough as they are, and therefore can be sure of their esteemed place.

Therefore, everyone is trying to be more, to be better, to reach higher. As a consequence, we are all neurotic in a neurotic society that pays a premium to the overly ambitious search for prestige and superiority. Underneath, we are all frightened people, not sure of ourselves, not sure of our worth, not sure of our place. It is this doubt of one's self, expressed in feelings of inadequacy and inferiority, which lies at the root of all maladjustment and all psychopathology.[3]

Jesus came into the world to save us from this very condition. To be released from such discontent represents redemption in its most profound form, and involves going all the way back to the very first thing that ever happened to us and changing the way we choose to perceive that event. We need to regard our own creation the way God regards *all* creation: as something "very, very good." This and this alone is the answer to the problem of "basic anxiety about one's self."

Agnes Sanford was the first person to introduce me to the intriguing concept of the "healing of the memories." She declares that the risen Christ is no more bounded by time than he is by space.[4] One of the effects of the resurrection is that now Jesus has access to every facet of creation—past, present, and future—as well as all places and spaces. What this means is that mercy has a potency that it never had before. The risen Lord is able to go back with us down the corridor of our memories, stop at each place of woundedness, and heal us as surely as he healed the lame and the blind during his earthly ministry.

Jesus cannot change the shape of the past, for there is a finality to yesterday that cannot be altered.

However, Jesus can change the meaning of those events for the present and future. They need no longer pour poison into our psyches, but by the grace of his healing touch, they can become springs of grace and wonder as we shift from thinking how bad we were to how good *God* is in being willing to forgive us. The deepest dimension of this "healing of the memories" goes all the way back to our births and transforms our perception of that event from something bad into something good.

Such an interpretation gives a new perspective to the phrase *being born again*. Jesus gives us a new way of perceiving the event of our own beginnings—and thus the whole of our lives. We, too, can begin to look on our creation the way Genesis depicts God as looking on all creation. When this begins to occur, delight rather than dissatisfaction becomes the lens through which all is perceived. The movement from "I'm OK" expands to include individuals, in-groups, out-groups, and finally all reality in a positive perspective. What begins with a new understanding of our own birth extends to the world itself, which means that the spirit of the petulant children—the essence of sin—is replaced by the spirit of the One who first looked on creation and pronounced it "good."

Author Sam Keen was raised in a little town in east Tennessee where his father taught in a small Presbyterian college. He claims that from early in his life he was engulfed by a sense of nobodiness—the feeling that as he was, he was not good enough. Like many of his contemporaries, he decided he had to go outside himself and import some significance to fill the emptiness within. Not surprisingly, academic achievement became his way of "trying to make something of himself." He did exceptionally well in

80

school. In fact, upon graduation from high school he was accepted into Harvard University. He had always thought that if he could ever attain such a goal, then his sense of nobodiness would evaporate and he would experience lasting positive self-esteem. He had not been at Harvard long, however, before the feelings of elation left, and he was back having to prove his worth once more through his accomplishments. He managed, once again, to do well and went on from Harvard to Princeton to work on a Ph.D. Alas, the satisfaction he had felt from graduating with honors turned out to be like "cotton candy"—a brief moment of sweetness, then nothing but emptiness in the mouth.

As Keen completed his graduate work at Princeton, he began to think that if he could get a job teaching and manage to publish a book, then a sense of well-being would finally be his. He proceeded to do both of these things, only to discover that he still was dominated by this sense of nobodiness. Everything came to a climax when he was invited to give a paper at one of the learned academic societies that meet during the Christmas holidays. He had dreamed of having the opportunity to do this, but after the experience he felt as empty as ever. He reports going back to his hotel room in Manhattan and getting down on his knees and crying out, "What must I do to be saved? How on earth can I find a sense of worth in the depths of my being?" As he cried out his despair, across the room, on the hotel wall, these words began to take shape. "Nothing! Nothing at all! It comes with the territory." At that moment he recalled the old image of a person "riding on an ox, and looking for an ox." Here was someone searching everywhere for something, and all along it was there underneath him, but he had never seen it before![5]

This is the truth Jesus came to reveal to every one of us. By the grace of God, we are what we are. Our worth is a gift given to us from the moment of our creation. The secret of our life in Christ is not getting something from outside to the inside by achieving. Instead, the secret is coming to recognize what is *already* inside by the grace of creation, and learning to bring this outside by sharing and serving. Thomas Merton calls this "the breakthrough to the Already."[6] It consists of seeing the first thing that ever happened to us—our birth—the way God sees it, and regarding it alongside God as something "very, very good!"

This way of seeing is the only antidote I know to the spirit of chronic dissatisfaction that characterized those children in Jesus' story and is still prevalent among us today. We can spend the rest of our lives asking "Where is Johnny's cap?" unless we allow the risen Lord to take us all the way down and all the way back so that we are truly able to reperceive the event of our birth. This is the beginning of seeing all things anew and aright, and also the beginning of grateful and joyful living.

81

Chapter Six

LOVE, FEAR, AND OUR NEIGHBOR

Just then a lawyer stood up to test Jesus. "Teacher," he said, "what must I do to inherit eternal life?" He said to him, "What is written in the law? What do you read there?" He answered, "You shall love the Lord your God with all your heart, and with all your soul, and with all your strength, and with all your mind; and your neighbor as yourself." And he said to him, "You have given the right answer; do this, and you will live."

But wanting to justify himself, he asked Jesus, "And who is my neighbor?" Jesus replied, "A man was going down from Jerusalem to Jericho, and fell into the hands of robbers, who stripped him, beat him, and went away, leaving him half dead. Now by chance a priest was going down that road; and when he saw him, he passed by on the other side.

So likewise a Levite, when he came to the place and saw him, passed by on the other side. But a Samaritan while traveling came near him; and when he saw him, he was moved with pity. He went to him and bandaged his wounds, having poured oil and wine on them. Then he put him on his own animal, brought him to an inn, and took care of him. The next day he took out two denarii, gave them to the innkeeper, and said, "Take care of him; and when I come back, I will repay you whatever more you spend." Which of these three, do you think, was a neighbor to the man who fell into the hands of the robbers?" He said, "The one who showed him mercy." Jesus said to him, "Go and do likewise."

Luke 10:25-37

Parables were often Jesus' way of diffusing conflictual situations and offering surprising insights that shifted the listener's perspective. This is the case with the most famous of all the stories he told—the one about the legendary good Samaritan.

The parable begins with a lawyer asking Jesus a question, a perennial question really: "What is life all about anyway?" Sometimes we put the issue this way: "What must I do to be saved?" At other times we ask, "How can I find my highest fulfillment?" or "What is the real reason for my existence?" This issue has been phrased in a variety of ways and represents a curiosity that is well-nigh universal. Who has not at times wondered what is involved in getting in touch with what is deepest and highest and most important in all existence?

Jesus responded to the lawyer the way any first-century rabbi would have done. He asked him, "What is written in the law? What do you read there?" This was vintage rabbinical procedure. I once asked a Jewish friend of mine why people of his faith often answer a question by asking another one. With a wry smile he replied, "Why not?" There is, of course, profound wisdom behind such a practice.

84

Jesus realized that most people are not just empty vessels into which one pours answers directly. If a truth is going to make any difference in a person's life, it is going to have to connect with where that person is already. Therefore, answering an inquiry by a further question is a way of probing the questioner more deeply, finding out exactly what is on their minds, and getting them involved in finding the answer they are seeking. This is a sound approach to authentic growth indeed, and precisely what Jesus chose to do.

The lawyer answered in words the Hebrew people had used for centuries in expressing their faith. "You shall love the Lord your God with all your heart, and with all your soul, and with all your strength, and with all your mind; and your neighbor as yourself." You will find these very words again and again throughout the Old Testament. They represent the Jewish vision of reality, and since this is the foundation of all that Jesus taught, let me emphasize just how seminal these words are.

From the biblical perspective, there are only two orders of reality: the Uncreated, which has life in itself, and the created, which derives its life from the other. This latter form is what we might call "contingent reality." It literally "hangs" like a chandelier. It *is* because Something Else has given it the right to be and caused it to be. Nothing but God belongs on the Uncreated side of the line, and everything except God belongs on the created side. Meister Eckhart put it succinctly when he wrote, "It is God's nature to give being. It is creation's nature to receive being."

Once we get this fundamental distinction clear, it is not surprising to find that we are to relate to these two orders in radically different ways. For example, we are to relate to the Uncreated—the already perfect and complete—by loving "with all our hearts and minds and souls and strength"; that is, we are to assume a stance of worship toward the One on whom we ultimately depend. We are to set that One in a category all alone, because there is nothing—absolutely nothing—exactly like the Lord our God, who is distinct from all other realities. Correspondingly, we are invited to love everything else on the created side of the line the way a parent loves a child, or the way a gardener loves the seed that she carefully husbands to its fulfillment. Everything that derives its life from the Creator is to be nurtured; only the Lord God is to be worshipped and recognized as an absolute.

If you and I could get the distinction between these two realities clear in our minds and learn to relate appropriately to each of them, this would be "the secret of eternal life," the key to fulfilling the destiny that was intended for us.

Our great problem here, however, is the issue of idolatry: we tend to take something that is on the created side of the line and relate to it as if it were the Uncreated. Whenever we take something that is not God and relate to it in a worshipful stance, expecting from it everything that we humans need, such behavior leads to profound disappointment. St. Augustine once prayed, "Thou hast made us for thyself, O God, and our hearts are restless until they rest in thee."

Mark it down that just as we can never get milk from a statue or wine from a stone, we can never get

85

our ultimate fulfillment from anything save our divine Source. Whatever is elevated to a place of worship on the created side of the line—be that a child, a job, a mate, or a possession—will inevitably leave us profoundly unfulfilled, for it is not that for which our hearts ultimately hunger. We were made to live worshipfully toward the Uncreated alone. We are never told to love our children "with all our hearts and minds and souls and strength." We are never told to love our parents or anything else, for that matter, in this way: only God is to be revered absolutely. Everything else is to be loved in such a way that encourages the creature to become what it has in it to be. God is already complete and is to be loved accordingly, while everything else is in the process of being completed. All of Jesus' teachings rest on this ancient understanding of reality. Although the Bible does not spell out "a plan of salvation," this would be it, should you decide to formulate one: "You shall love the LORD your God with all your heart, soul, and strength, and love your neighbor as yourself."

I remember years ago I had a young parishioner who went away to college. Like so many of his contemporaries, he had been taught the faith all his life but was really not all that interested in it. When he got to college, however, he encountered an intense group of fundamentalists and had a profound religious experience of his own. He came back "with fire in his eyes" saying, "Why haven't I ever heard the gospel before? My parents and my church don't know anything about the Lord." He felt he was absolutely superior to everybody else because of his newfound experience.

I have seen many adolescents go through this phase. I always celebrate what they have discovered and am patient with their accusations. I understand that as they continue on the Way, things are not going to stay as simple as they appear to them in those beginning moments. I knew the college freshman was going to need me later on, and sure enough, six months later he was back in my study in great distress.

"I've been reading the Bible a lot lately," he told me. "This group that I am with says there is only one way—a single plan for salvation—but I can't find it as I read the scriptures. Jesus talks out of all sides of his mouth, it seems. For example, Nicodemus came to him to ask what he must do to be saved, and Jesus told him that he had to be born again. But when the woman by the well in Samaria encountered Jesus, he told her she needed to drink of the living water that would quench her thirst in an ultimate way. And when the rich young ruler comes with the same desire and the same question, Jesus does not say anything about being born again or drinking living water, but instead commands him to go and sell what he has, give it away to the poor, and follow him. Where is the one plan of salvation?"

"That is a very good question," I replied. "What you need to realize is that there is a common foundation underneath all these prescriptions. Jesus was like any good physician: he did not prescribe the same medicine for every patient who walked through the door. He proportioned the medication to the particular sickness he detected. The one plan of salvation is this: 'You shall love the Lord your God with all your heart, mind, soul and strength.' Yet this had to be applied to the unique idolatries of each individual. For example, Nicodemus was a Jewish leader, a person who probably prized above all else that he had been born into this world a physical descendant of Abraham. He had taken something on the created side of the line and was treating it as if it were the Uncreated, which is why Jesus challenged him as he did: 'You need to rethink this matter of being born all over again. It is the fact that you are a son of God, not a son of Abraham, that ought to matter most.'"

"In the case of the Samaritan woman, however, the shape of her idolatry was quite different. She may have made sensuality and feeling the central focus in her life, which meant she needed to experience God as the source of her delight, rather than anything in the created realm. The rich young ruler, on the other hand, did not worship his Jewishnesss nor his feelings. It was his material possessions that had gotten over on the Uncreated side of the line. This is why Jesus said to him that he needed to give away that on which he had come to depend and begin to trust the Maker of all things. The ruler had confused the means by which he lived for the End for whom he should live. Jesus invited him to shift his ultimate allegiance."

I tried to help this young man see that there *is* a single plan of salvation, but it has to be applied to the shape of each person's particular idolatry. If you comb the gospels carefully, you will discover that Jesus talked about the first law of Moses more than all the other nine put together. We are to have no other gods before the only God there is—or, to put it another way, we are to love our Source as we love nothing else, and to love the rest of creation with the kind of nurturing affection that enables it to grow. Therefore, when Jesus heard the lawyer formulate the classic Hebrew vision, he applauded him: "You've got it! That is it in a nutshell. All you have to do is to put this vision into practice, and you will inherit eternal life. The secret is yours. Go and live your life accordingly."

The lawyer, however, apparently had other things on his agenda beyond finding out truth for himself. After all, the beginning of the passage says that he was testing Jesus. Thus, after Jesus helped him to see that he already knew the answer to the question he was asking, the lawyer, instead of embracing that and going out to live it, attempted to save face by asking a further question. "Just a minute. Exactly who is my neighbor?"

I sense the lawyer was doing something here that I have often done myself. You see, I have two very different forms of needs. There are times in my life when I am so confused that I do not know how to put my left foot in front of my right foot. What I need in those moments are some words of direction and guidance. There are other times, however, when I know exactly what I am supposed to do, but I do not want to do it, or do not have the energy to do it, or somehow do not have the courage to put it into practice. And the truth is, I am not above hiding behind the first to avoid the second, of spinning out complexities when in fact the issue is action and not confusion.

This is what I see the lawyer doing here. It had really become clear what he was supposed to do: he was to love God in one way and the rest of creation in another. Yet rather than putting his energies toward actualizing this ideal, he resorted to a delaying tactic and raised another complex issue. "Exactly who is my neighbor?" the man wanted to know.

The question has been debated in every age: How is the identity of a neighbor to be defined? The lawyer was really asking, "How far does my responsibility go here? What, in fact, constitutes neighborness, and who qualifies to receive the love called for in the law?" He might have been asking, "What is the least I am required to do to get by?"

Laws evoke this kind of attitude. When it comes time to pay our income tax, for example, we want to obey the law but do not want to pay one more cent than is required. At this point Jesus realized, I think, that he was up against somebody who was not just seeking the truth. Here was a complex man with all kinds of issues at work on several levels of his life. And so, instead of giving him a direct answer, Jesus proceeded to tell him this parable.

When people heard Jesus say, "A man was going down from Jerusalem to Jericho," they knew this to be literally true. The city of Jerusalem is on the highest elevation in Palestine, some 2300 feet above sea level, while Jericho is down by the Dead Sea at the lowest place on this planet, some 1300 feet below sea level. Thus, in the span of a very few miles, there is a precipitous drop. The road, like all mountain ways, was quite circuitous and narrow, with desert on either side. To this day, it is known as the "Red and Bloody Way" because so much violence has occurred there. It was easy for robbers to slip in from the desert, assault and rob somebody, and then disappear back into the desert. The very thing Jesus described was commonplace on this road and utterly familiar to his audience.

Thus, Jesus told of a man being robbed and left there, beaten and half-dead. Three familiar figures passed by where the stricken man was lying. Each one of them would have been easily recognizable to a Palestinian audience. There was a priest of the temple who represented religion at its professional best, a man who had been given the responsibility of not only presiding over the sacrifices but also of keeping

90

alive the traditions of Israel. Second was a Levite, who was a lower-level temple functionary. He, too, had the responsibility of carrying on the traditions of the Hebrews.

The third person making his way by the helpless man was identified as "a Samaritan." Residents of the region of Samaria, the Samaritans practiced a heretical version of Judaism and were racially distinct from Jews. First-century Jews regarded them as a loathsome and churlish people. Because Samaritans were ostracized and widely regarded as worthless, they often lived up to this cultural expectation and acted as if they had no worth. Folk of that day would not have expected anything humane, or heroic, or compassionate from a Samaritan. In fact, they probably would have surmised that a Samaritan would go over and try to plunder the already beaten victim.

The most distinctive thing about a parable, remember, is the element of surprise. Jesus' story had the lawyer so enthralled that his defenses were down. Precisely at that moment, Jesus shocked the life out of him by saying it was the Samaritan—not the priest or the Levite—who reacted humanely, even heroically, in that situation. The Samaritan was the one to stop, go over to the stricken man, and do what he could to help him. He put him on his own beast of burden and took him to the nearest inn where the wounded man would have long-term care—and he paid for this out of his own pocket.

Here is an incredible example of "loving your neighbor." It came from a person that no one in that society would have expected to be capable of such compassion. All the hearers, not just the lawyer, must have been astonished. Jesus asked, "Which one of these three, do you think, was neighbor to the man who was in need?" Once again, the answer was obvious—the one who showed pity. Then Jesus said, "Go and do likewise."

It is important to notice what Jesus did with the lawyer's question, "Who is my neighbor?" He turned it around 180 degrees and focused it on the lawyer, not on anyone else. There was a long tradition among Jesus' people of finding ways to limit their liabilities. Again and again this term "neighbor" was trimmed to smaller and smaller proportions; for example, only those who were descended from Abraham or who had property were considered neighbors.

However, Jesus turned in the other direction altogether and said, "You are to think of yourself as a neighbor." The question is not, "Is such and such a person worthy of my love?" but rather, "Am I willing to take what I have, what I know, and what I can do and place all this at the disposal of another person's needs or growth?"

We need to remember that creation comes out of God's generosity and that we humans are made in that image. Thus, what the Samaritan did on the Jericho road was to act out what it means to be made in the image of primal generosity. Loving one's neighbor is making a gift of what we have been given by God. "Loving our neighbors as ourselves" answers to the deepest impulses within us. We love because it is our nature to love. We do not ask, "Are they worthy?" but rather, "Am I willing to act out the image of God that is within?"

What keeps us from acting out of our highest and best identities? In terms of the parable, why was it the Samaritan, not the priest or Levite, who stopped to help the stricken man? Let us ponder the dynamics of our own hearts as we ask these probing questions.

It could be a matter of courage. The priest and Levite may have allowed fear to dehumanize them. They had an innate sense of compassion, I imagine, like everyone else, but when they saw the beaten man and realized where they were—the Red and Bloody Way—all their high ideals and religious motivations evaporated. Fear does cast out love. It contracts our vision to ourselves and ourselves alone. Perhaps this fear accounts for otherwise good men deciding to do nothing except run for their own lives. The Samaritan, on the other hand, might have been in touch with the reality that is greater than fear: love. Love is what enables a person to cast out fear and create courage. Paul Tillich used to claim that courage was the foundational virtue, and that we are not likely to get very far in loving God, our neighbors, or ourselves unless we are empowered by it.

Then again, perhaps the three men acted differently on the Red and Bloody Way because of time pressure. Realize, if you will, that the priest and Levite might have had obligations at the temple to fulfill. The Samaritan, on the other hand, might not have been so tightly committed. Thus, he had a freedom to respond spontaneously to the unexpected in ways that the highly structured priest and Levite could not.

Years ago I heard of an interesting experiment that was conducted to ascertain what factors enabled people to act lovingly and what factors worked against the same thing. A seminary professor recruited fifteen volunteers from his class to meet him at his office at two o'clock. When they arrived, he handed out sealed instructions. Five of the envelopes instructed the recipients to proceed across the campus without delay. They were told, "You have fifteen minutes to reach this place. You have no time to spare. Do not loiter or do anything else, or your grade will be docked." These five were coded "The High Hurry Group." The next five were instructed that, anytime in the next forty-five minutes, they were to make their way across the campus. "You will have plenty of time," they were told, "but don't be too slow." They were coded "The Medium Hurry Group." The last five were told that, any time before five o'clock that afternoon, they were to report across campus, and there they would receive further instructions. This group was known as "The Low Hurry Group."

Unbeknownst to any of these students, the professor had arranged with some drama majors at Princeton University to be situated alongside the path they had to take, simulating great human needfulness. One was sitting with his head in his hands, crying and wailing in a way one could not ignore. Another was lying face down, as if he had had some kind of seizure and was unconscious. Still another was shaking violently as if he were about to throw up. All fifteen of the students had to make their way past these obviously needy persons, and here is what happened.

None of "The High Hurry Group" stopped to see what they could do, although all five of them aspired to become Christian ministers. Two of "The Medium Hurry Group" stopped to try to help, and all five of "The Low Hurry Group" made attempts to be responsive. The point that emerged out of the exercise was that *pressure is a moral category.* Any time we get ourselves over-booked or have too many irons in the fire, it affects our ability to respond to the unanticipated. No matter how lofty our idealism, when our date book is filled to the hilt, it shapes what we are moved to do.

This might well have been the problem for the priest and the Levite, while perhaps the Samaritan was more realistic. Maybe the Samaritan had learned that his limits were as real a part of him as his gifts. What he could *not* do said as much about how God had made him as what he could do. Whether or not this was the reason, here is something for all of us to consider: Do our busy lives keep us from being what we really want to be? Raw evil is not the only temptation most of us face. At times, the good can become an enemy of the best, especially when we take on too many "good causes" and forget our limits.

A third possibility to explain how this parable unfolded could be that the overly judgmental attitude on the part of the priest and Levite simply was not shared by the Samaritan. Perhaps on seeing this beaten man, the first two said to themselves, "He was foolish to have been traveling alone with items of value. Everybody knows that if you are carrying precious cargo, you need to travel this way in caravans, not by yourself." Therefore, they might have rationalized their way out of doing anything on the grounds that the victim deserved his fate because of his own foolishness. "He made his bed—now let him lie in it," they might have reasoned.

On the other hand, perhaps the Samaritan was more immediate and less analytical in the way he saw the situation. His attitude might have been "Need justifies ministry." He probably would not have argued that we need to look into the reasons why bad things happen to good people. Once a person is robbed and beaten and lying by the side of the road, elaborate speculation on how he got there is secondary to doing something about his wounds.

I once saw a sign that read, "Yes, I'd like to help you out. Show me how you came in." It smacked of evading help by resorting to analysis. There is a place for this sort of thing, but it ought to come after the oil and bandages and wine have been applied. Perhaps the Samaritan realized that we humans never know enough to judge another person absolutely, but we do know enough to take what we have and place it at the disposal of another's need. God never asks any of us to occupy the seat of judgment, but he does call us to wash each other's feet and do what we can to be of practical help. In doing this, which was certainly not all that needed to be done, the Samaritan was clearly superior to the two who decided to do nothing.

A fourth reason why the Samaritan stopped to help might have been that he alone had with him certain things that matched the needs of that moment. After all, Jesus did mention oil and wine and a donkey, all of which the Samaritan readily shared. It is entirely possible that given their professions, the priest and Levite carried none of these things with them. Thus, when they saw the man and realized his dire needs, they decided the best thing they could do was go as quickly as possible to get him appropriate help. If this is why they swiftly "passed by on the other side," I would say their response was as loving as that of the Samaritan.

The point here is that we are never called on to give what we do not have, or to do things for people that we are not capable of doing. It is important to recognize that our response to people involves more than just their needs. The particular shape of our giftedness is a determinant as well. It would be irresponsible to rush into situations where we do not have the ability to be part of the answer. If you are having an attack of appendicitis, it would be criminal for me to try to resolve that problem. At that moment, you need the services of a competent surgeon.

I was stopped at a red light some time ago and noticed a car on the other side of the busy thoroughfare. A middle-aged woman was helplessly looking under the hood. She was obviously stalled and did not know what to do. I decided to try to help, but let me describe the form that my helpfulness assumed. I do not know the first thing about auto mechanics. If I had gotten under that hood and tried to remedy the problem, I would have probably made it worse. So instead, I pulled over and offered to go to a service station two blocks away to find help.

When I suggested this, she beamed and said, "That would be wonderful."

"Is there anybody I can call for you?" I asked.

"Would you mind telephoning Rita at the Bon Ton Beauty Shop and telling her that my car is on the blink and I'm going to be late?" she replied.

The two things that I could do, I did with dispatch. Perhaps the differential in the parable, then, is one of hard practicalities: the Samaritan had with him what was needed; the priest and Levite did not. If they hastened to get appropriate help, they were just as faithful as the Samaritan. We need to be careful, lest we make love look like doing the impossible. It really consists of doing what you can with what you have for the help or growth of another. You do not have to have a Ph.D. to love your neighbor.

The last possibility is that the Samaritan stopped because he was a Samaritan, and a very special one at that. Remember that Samaritans were racially distinct from and roundly disliked by Jesus' people. Given this special historical burden, they tended to respond to their destiny in one of three ways. Most

Samaritans simply gave up in the face of all this hostility, crept to the sidelines, and lived out their days in quiet despair. The majority of Samaritans were deeply depressed people. A smaller group of Samaritans took the opposite approach. They were enraged at the injustice of treating persons this way and became revolutionaries, ready to do whatever they could to overthrow the establishment and to give their oppressors a taste of their own medicine. But the trouble was, there were so few Samaritans in relation to the Jews and the Romans that whenever they turned to violence, they were the ones who wound up getting hurt.

However there was yet a third round of Samaritans, the smallest in number, but arguably the most admirable in their approach. These were the Samaritans who took the injustices of their experience in history and somehow transmuted this into awareness and sensitivity to other suffering people. They also developed a compassion that wanted to keep others from being hurt as they had been hurt. It could be that the Samaritan in Jesus' story was just such a special sufferer. Here was a man who knew from his own experience what it was like to be beaten and left by the side of the road. He was no stranger to this sort of harsh treatment. However, instead of giving up in despair or blowing up in rage, this Samaritan had somehow transmuted his suffering into something higher: he was moved to help.

There is no way to prove that this is the proper explanation, but to me it is the most heroic. Of all the things that I would like to do with my days and nights, I can think of nothing more appealing than becoming one who chooses to take his wounds and transpose them into awareness, sensitivity, and compassion. I do not think there are many persons among us who have had the same kind of injustices perpetrated on them as had the Samaritans, but if every one of us could tell his or her own story, we have all had things happen to us that we cannot understand. We have all lost people whom we loved and we have all tasted bitter disappointments. We, too, have been tempted to respond to these hurts by giving up on life and becoming bitter and angry people. But there is always this alternative: to turn our wounds into the desire to bless and help; to become what Henri Nouwen called "wounded healers." And, for me at least, there is no higher goal or aspiration.

I admit, then, that among all the possibilities there is no conclusive answer to the question of why it was the Samaritan, and not the priest or the Levite, who stopped and loved this bruised neighbor. But the point is, the Samaritan did it—and so can we.

Go, then, and do likewise!

Chapter Seven

A MIDNIGHT REQUEST

Suppose one of you has a friend, and you go to him at midnight and say to him: "Friend, lend me three loaves of bread; for a friend of mine has arrived, and I have nothing to set before him." And he answers from within, "Do not bother me; the door has already been locked, and my children are with me in bed; I cannot get up and give you anything." I tell you, even though he will not get up and give him anything because he is his friend, at least because of his persistence he will get up and give him whatever he needs.

But I say to you, Ask, and it will be given you; search, and you will find; knock, and the door will be opened for you. For everyone who asks receives, and for everyone who searches finds, and for every-one who knocks, the door will be opened. Is there anyone among you who, if your child asks for a fish, will give a snake instead of a fish? Or if the

child asks for an egg, will give him a scorpion? If you then, who are evil, know how to give good gifts to your children, how much more will the heavenly Father give the Holy Spirit to those who ask him!
Luke 11:5-13

The longer I live, the more convinced I become that there are only two basic realities—love and fear. At the functional level, love is the perception that we humans are created in the image of an abundant One, and that what we already have is adequate to meet any crises we might confront. This sense of sufficiency is the source of what my friend Charles Boddie used to call "cope-ability"—the courage to deal resourcefully with whatever occurs.

Fear, however, is at the opposite end of this continuum. It is the perception that there is not enough and never will be—not enough knowledge, not enough power, not enough love. This means that one is always outmatched by reality—up against the overpowering—and such a perception does destructive things all the way around.

If it is true that love has the power to cast out fear, as the writer of 1 John affirms (4:18), it is equally true that fear has the power to cast out love. I am never less loving than when I am most afraid. Fear turns all of us into egocentric monsters, unable to think of anything but ourselves and prone to all sorts of destructive behavior or complete indifference to the plight of others. Fear is the great unmaking of the highest and the best in human beings. This fact highlights the importance of learning to perceive reality in terms of abundance rather than scarcity.

What occurs on the perceptional level is what shapes our behavior. This is precisely where Jesus chose to do his redemptive work and why parables like this one of the neighbor's midnight request are of such seminal importance. Here Jesus speaks directly to the issue of Ultimate Reality. What is the mystery behind it all really like? To whom exactly do we address our prayers? In the words of this parable, Jesus provides us a powerful and hopeful answer.

Anyone, even a child, could understand Jesus. The details of this parable reflect very accurately the way first-century Galilean peasants lived. It needs to be remembered that back in those days, people traveled largely on foot. Because of the excessive heat, the accepted practice was to start out late in the afternoon and walk into the first part of the night. So it was not at all unusual that at midnight, an unexpected relative might appear at the door asking for hospitality. We also need to realize that there were very few public inns in that era, which is why hospitality was regarded as such a virtue. It was the only way that poor people could travel and survive.

Thus, if a person had to make a journey, he would often plot his course carefully in order to get to Cousin George's tonight and Aunt Sarah's tomorrow night. On the hosting end, it was common courtesy to give a weary traveler something to eat, no matter how late he arrived. That is precisely the context of Jesus' little story.

A friend arrived in the dead of the night and the host found himself without sufficient food. Peasants in that day lived very close to the edge. There was rarely much of a surplus of anything. Rather than embarrass himself, however, and send his guest to bed hungry, the host excused himself, ventured next door, and asked his neighbor if he could bail him out by giving him three loaves—enough for an average family meal of that time. The response of the man next door was utterly typical.

Again, one needs to realize that most peasant houses were one-room enclosures. Many of them did not have windows. There was usually a single door that afforded access both inside and out, a dirt floor, some kind of stove against a wall, and pegs on which people could hang things. The cooking was done outside; in fact, almost everything was done outside. The houses were basically sleeping places. After supper the father would gather up his tools and his animals and move them inside. Then he would call in his wife and children and close the door. He would bank the fire, put a bushel over the lamp to keep it from blowing out, and then they would lie down together on the dirt floor, the children closest to the stove. It would be totally dark inside.

The accepted courtesy was that you did not bother a neighbor once the closing rituals of the day had occurred. This accounts for the initial response to the neighbor's request. A voice from within responded sleepily. "Can't you see that the door is shut? Don't you know that my children are in bed with me?" That was literally the case: they were all around him on the dirt floor, and it was utterly dark. "I can't get up and give you bread at this time of night. It would wake up the whole neighborhood!"

I must pause at this point and acknowledge empathy for this poor man. I remember what it was like as a parent finally to get the children down for the night. I imagine that little ones in every age have attempted to string out going to bed as long as possible. For example, my children developed incredible thirsts and an insatiable desire for stories about nine o'clock each night. My son, who is now in his forties, was particularly skilled in extending this process. When I was absolutely worn out, he would plead, "Tell me about Jesus." What was a minister to do?

103

How can you turn your back on that kind of open door to religious instruction? It was all a ruse, of course, to stay awake as long as he could. The eleventh commandment at our house was: "Never wake a sleeping child!" There were no crises severe enough to justify starting the going-to-bed ritual all over again. Therefore, I feel for this drowsy neighbor; the canons of common courtesy had been violated.

The embarrassed host, however, was not willing to give up easily. He kept on knocking at the door until, I suppose, the children were awakened. By this time, the whole inside was a sea of turmoil. The neighbor, probably saying under his breath, "Anything to get rid of that loudmouth from next door," got up, took the bushel off the lamp, went to the cupboard, fetched what the neighbor was requesting, and sullenly handed it over. Persistence won out over reluctance. One man went home happy while another household was left in shambles.

This is a story that Jesus told in response to the request, "Teach us to pray," but quite frankly, for years I have been troubled by the whole thing. The surface meaning seems to suggest that persistence is the key to authentic praying. If we keep at it long enough, we finally wear God out and God says, "Okay, okay, since I cannot get rid of you in any other way, I am going to give you what you are asking."

Such an image is hardly an appealing theological vision. It seems to reverse the Creator/creature relationship altogether. It gives the pushiest among us the upper hand and the final say, which is not reassuring at all. Thus, for a long period this was a closed passage for me.

Then one day, someone pointed out to me a linguistic detail that shifted my whole perspective. It was that the common conjunction in Greek, *kai,* can be translated either "and," "so," or "but" depending on the context. "And" and "so" link together things that are in continuity with each other, while "but" signals a shift in direction. "But" is an introduction to contrast, not continuation, and translating the conjunction at the beginning of the ninth verse as "but" rather than "so" gives the story a totally new twist. Hence, "he will get up and give him whatever he needs. But I say to you, Ask, and it will be given you...."

It suddenly dawned on me that this notion of persistence winning out over reluctance was the pagan notion of prayer, not the vision Jesus came to give. He was putting here in story form what fear had done to the human understanding of God. Had not the serpent in the garden of Eden suggested that God was not good and could not be trusted? Had he not implied that there was finally not enough in the Holy One, so that life was a game of "everyone for himself"?

If you are at all conversant with the literature of paganism, you will recall that the hallmark of pagan divinities was their indifference to the human plight, even their downright hostility to the creatures of earth. The great sadness in those parts of the world that have never been touched by the biblical story of a blessing God is rooted in the belief that there is nothing that really cares for us at all, or if Something does care, it cares only in very negative ways.

One of the most famous pagan myths is about a lesser god named Prometheus. One day he looked down from Mount Olympus and saw human beings stumbling around in the dark and the cold. Somehow this situation evoked compassion in him. He took some fire from the altar of heaven and brought it down to the human race that they might be illumined and warmed. When Zeus, however, discovered what Prometheus had done, he was furious. Prometheus had violated one of the laws of heaven, which was that no god should feel compassion for earth. Therefore, Prometheus was punished by being chained to a rock with a vulture eating endlessly at his insides.

This myth is a metaphor for the deep aversion it was believed heaven had for earth. It puts into picture-language the way paganism felt about the divine reality. What happened to humans simply did not matter to the gods. In this sense, the awakened neighbor who has no sympathy for this crisis of hospitality embodies the pagan understanding of the gods. It also follows that the persistent wearing down of another represents the pagan understanding of prayer.

We would make a great mistake, however, to relegate such attitudes to ancient times and distant cultures. Unless you are very different from me, I dare say you will find elements of this same sort of fearfulness deep inside you. For example, when you hear the term "the will of God," is your first reaction one of elation and intrigue, or apprehension and uneasiness? What do you honestly think would happen if you did turn your whole life over to God? Would things get better or worse than they are now?

I heard once of a little boy who was asked in Sunday school, "What do you think God is like?" His response was, "God is the Great Killjoy. He always has a frown on his face as he walks around. If he finds anybody having a good time, he puts a stop to it as quickly as possible."

In all honesty, is such an image completely foreign to the way we feel at the deepest level? We may not voice such uneasiness about the nature of divinity openly, but my sense is that for most of us it lies buried in our subconscious. These apprehensions have been alive and well in me at times, and I do not think I am alone. Many people have acknowledged to me that they believe if they ever did open the door to God, God would promptly demand that they give up everything they enjoy.

Let me suggest that this is precisely the place where Jesus came to do the work of reconciliation, and this parable is one of his instruments. Having given graphic expression to the fearful image of God in the guise of the neighbor, he then spoke dramatically: "But I say to you, Ask, and it will be given you; search, and you will find; knock, and the door will be opened for you." And then in poetic parallelism, he repeated those same truths: "For everyone who asks receives, and for everyone who searches finds, and for everyone who knocks, the door will be opened."

By that contrast, Jesus set an utterly different image of God over against the fears of the ages. The neighbor was not a mirror image of the true God, but the antithesis. To drive the point home, Jesus describes the way a healthy parent responds to a child: "Is there anyone among you who, if your child asks for a fish, will give a snake instead of a fish? Or if the child asks for an egg, will give him a scorpion?" He went on: "If you then, who are evil, know how to give good gifts to your children, how much more will the heavenly Father give the Holy Spirit to those who ask him!" You see, to the mystery of Godness, Jesus gave a face, and on that face he put a smile—the expression of a loving parent—which is another way of saying that Jesus ultimately opened the way for love to cast out fear and for a sense of sufficiency to take the place of a sense of not enough.

When this transformation happens at the deepest level, then prayer ceases to be a pressing against reluctance and becomes rather a confident sharing with One who already cares. Herein lies the secret of "cope-ability." A person can face up to any and all eventualities if her sense of the Ultimate One is that of abundance and adequacy.

I was privileged as a little child to be exposed to a human being in whom Jesus really had effected this shift from fearfulness to love. She was an old African-American woman named Gladys Meggs who worked and lived in our home for almost a decade. I remember she was always cheerful and full of life. If you asked her why this was so, Gladys would say, "Ain't nothin' going to happen today that me and Jesus can't handle!"

That is good theology, and precisely the sort of mind-set this little parable was meant to convey. We do not pray to One who slumbers in indifference. No, we pray to One who gives us more than we can ask or expect—God's very self in the Holy Spirit—because that is God's nature as our loving Parent.

There is, then, enough—always has been and always will be—and realizing this makes all the difference in the world!

Chapter Eight

THE RICH FOOL

Someone in the crowd said to him, "Teacher, tell my brother to divide the family inheritance with me." But he said to him, "Friend, who set me to be a judge or arbitrator over you?" And he said to them, "Take care! Be on your guard against all kinds of greed; for one's life does not consist in the abundance of possessions." Then he told them a parable: "The land of a rich man produced abundantly. And he thought to himself, 'What should I do, for I have no place to store my crops?' Then he said, 'I will do this: I will pull down my barns and build larger ones, and there I will store all my grain and my goods. And I will say to my soul, 'Soul, you have ample goods laid up for many years; relax, eat, drink, be merry.' But God said to him, 'You fool! This very night your life is being demanded of you. And the things you have prepared, whose will they be?' So it is with those who store up treasures for themselves but are not rich toward God."

Luke 12:13-21

Peter deVries, the novelist who once considered becoming a minister himself, wrote a funny novel in which one of the characters is a very liberal Unitarian minister who prides himself on being as abstract and esoteric as possible. The minister is particularly pleased with himself one Sunday when he begins his sermon by saying, "It is an aspect of God's omnipotence that He can save us without having to exist."[1]

If asked, I would wager that none of the listeners that day had the slightest idea what that string of words really meant. In contrast, if you look deeply at the stories of Jesus, you will not encounter the kind of verbal abstraction that goes over our heads or in and out of our ears. His parables invariably touch us where we live or hurt or experience some need.

Such uncanny insight is evident in this parable where Jesus, teaching the multitudes, is suddenly interrupted by a man who is obviously quite upset. "Teacher, make my brother divide our inheritance with me." Disputes about inheritances were very common in that time, for the social arrangement of the family dictated that the oldest son assumed control the moment his father died, and he acquired the responsibility for settling the estate with all the other siblings.

In Jesus' story of the prodigal son, the older brother probably got a two-thirds share, simply by virtue of his birth order, while the prodigal got only one-third. If there were more than two children, the oldest son probably would have received one half of the estate and everyone else would have received a portion of what was left. The point is that first-born sons occupied exceedingly powerful positions in ancient family systems. This explains why in the Old

Testament story of Esau and Jacob there was such a tremendous struggle over who was going to get the family blessing and birthright. In that case, the two were twins but since Esau had come out of the womb ahead of Jacob, he was the eldest. Therefore, by the custom of that time, most of the power and resources went to Esau, and Jacob was faced with having to circumvent tradition in order to get the role of leadership for which he was actually more gifted and capable.

I began my active ministry in a wonderful little southern town in middle Tennessee. One of the great things about living in such a place was hearing all the stories that comprised the heritage of the community. One such tale was about the president of a bank whose two sons were the reverse of the prodigal and his elder brother. In this case, the older son was a fun-loving rake, while the younger brother was a responsible, straight-arrow type who always played by the rules. When their father died, the two brothers found themselves alone in the funeral parlor with their father's corpse.

"You and I both know that money meant more to our father than anything else," said the older son. "I think the most appropriate thing for us to do at this moment would be for each of us to put a thousand dollars in his hands and let it be buried with him. What more apt tribute could we pay to him?"

"Of course, that would be appropriate," responded the straight-arrow brother.

The story has it that he went to the bank, got ten crisp one-hundred-dollar bills, and put them carefully into his dead father's hand. Later that night, when nobody else was around, the older brother came, took the thousand dollars, wrote a check for two thousand dollars and slipped it into his father's hand!

The point is, if you had that kind of older brother in the first century, you too would be looking for somebody like Jesus to intervene and give you some help!

This is precisely the context in which Luke sets the parable of the rich fool. An older brother must have been dragging his feet when it came to dividing the family inheritance, and a younger sibling attempts to get Jesus involved in the process because there was no court system in that day to handle such family conflicts. Interestingly enough, Jesus' response is curtly negative. He chooses not to get sucked into this family fracas.

This is one of three occasions in the gospels when someone asked Jesus to do something to a third party. In all three cases, he refused to reinforce such a manipulative way of dealing with problems. You remember the time when Martha was working busily in the kitchen while her sister Mary was sitting in the living room talking with Jesus (Luke 10:38-42). Martha got upset enough to demand that Jesus tell Mary that her place was in the kitchen helping with the meal. Jesus did not go along with such a ploy. Instead, he called on the accuser to deal with her own issues. Jesus never encouraged people to attempt to solve their problems by going behind the backs of others.

The third occasion was the day the scribes and the Pharisees brought a woman to the temple who had been caught in the very act of adultery (John 8:1-11). These individuals were very clear about what they thought the law of Moses taught them to do in such situations. Yet when they attempted to involve Jesus in the affair, he refused to join them in their condemnation, turning the focus rather on their sins instead.

In the same fashion, we find Jesus choosing not to deal with the complaint of the man in our story by siding with him against his brother. His approach was always to reinforce the idea that people should take responsibility for their own actions and their own lives. We are never told to go to God and focus our attention on the offenses of others. When we go to God, we need to go with our own baggage, our own "sack of rocks." We need to deal with the log in our own eye rather than the speck in someone else's eye. We best go to God as grateful people or as confessors, not as complainers or accusers.

There might have been, however, a deeper reason why Jesus refused to do what the man in our story asked of him. He might have sensed in the man's body language or in his urgency to get the matter settled that the real issue here was not justice at all, but a spirit of covetousness. At any rate, he responded by saying, "Take care! Be on your guard against all kinds of greed; for one's life does not consist in the abundance of possessions." Again and again in the gospels, Jesus demonstrates a good nose for idolatry. He had more to say about the first commandment of Moses than all the other nine put together: "I am the LORD your God...; you shall have no other gods before me" (Exodus 20:2-3). Jesus was very sensitive to our human tendency to elevate something that is not God into godlike status. My hunch is that this is what Jesus detected behind the younger brother's concern, so he proceeded to deal with him far differently from the way the man had expected.

You see, idolatry is no surface or incidental matter. It can lead to devastating consequences. In one of his lectures, Samuel Miller, former dean of Harvard Divinity School, told of being in Munich in 1931 when German culture was flourishing. One night he went to the Bavarian National Opera House to see one of the last of what he called "The Metaphysical Clowns," a man named Karl Valentino. Charlie Chaplin would be a popular example of such a performer—a person who dressed like a clown and did clown-like pantomimes, but actually was conveying profound truth through his art.

114

The pantomime began with a stage that was bare except for one circle of light. The clown entered that circle and began to search very diligently for something he had lost. After a time, a policeman came up and asked, "Have you lost something?"

"The key to my house," replied the clown. "If I can't find it, I can't go home tonight."

With that, the policeman joined in the search with great intensity. Finally he asked, "Are you sure you lost it here?"

"Oh, no, I lost it over there," said the clown, pointing to a darkened part of the stage.

"Then why on earth are you looking here?"

"Because there is no light over there."

Such an exchange may seem terribly foolish on a superficial level, but beneath the action Miller saw a profound symbol of human futility. To look for something where it does not exist is the ultimate formula for disappointment. This, in truth, is what we do in an act of idolatry.

When we look for an encounter with the Ultimate where ultimacy does not exist, we inevitably fail. Jesus must have sensed that this was what the man was doing. By asking Jesus to help him get his inheritance, he was really thinking that the material sector of reality encompassed all he needed to come to total fulfillment. Perhaps the real problem was not with the older brother at all, but with the younger one's confused understanding of reality itself. This is why

Jesus told him to beware of all greed, for "one's life does not consist in the abundance of possessions."

Let me underline that Jesus was never simplistic in the way he dealt with the material realm. Philosophically, there have always been economic absolutists on both ends of the continuum. There are people who say that the material realm is all there is, there being no other kind of reality except the realm of things. At the other extreme, there are those who say that wealth, in and of itself, is evil and that any kind of private property or possession is lethal to the human spirit.

Jesus, however, was never an oversimplifier: he did not identify with either of these extremes. His attitude toward the material dimension of life seemed to be one of sanity and balance. He did not take a vow of poverty, for example. Proof of this is the fact that he was often accused of being a "glutton and a drunkard" (Luke 7:34), of loving the good things of life too much. He never said that simply possessing something was an evil in itself. When he was arrested at the end of his life, he was wearing a seamless robe—a fine and valuable garment—and he numbered many wealthy individuals among his best friends. One of his heroes, the good Samaritan, was obviously well-to-do, having resources out of which he was able to act redemptively.

I think Jesus would say that possessing private property can help individuals in their moral development. Think about it. How can you ever become a responsible individual if you never have anything for which to be responsible? If you never let people experience ownership of any kind, all they will ever know is infantile dependency. There is no way to develop a sense of responsibility apart from having something for which to be responsible. To say to a child, "Learn to read, and then I will give you a book," or "Learn to swim, and then I will let you go into the water," is a counsel of futility indeed. We have to have something that is our own in order to learn how to be responsible stewards.

I believe that Jesus understood this fact, which is why you do not find him saying either that wealth was everything or that wealth was evil. What Jesus did say quite clearly was that the material order can do certain things for us, and that it cannot do other things. It does not possess all of the resources that we need to be fulfilled as human beings. If we place any material object on the altar of ultimate importance, hoping to extract from it everything that feeds the hungers of our heart, we are going to be sorely disappointed.

When I wrote earlier that Jesus had a good nose for idolatry, I meant that he could sense when someone was expecting too much from a given reality, and he was quick to warn of such a mistake. This is what we see him doing here with the man who was so upset about his inheritance. He was calling him to the realization that what a person *has* does not define what a person *is*.

After warning his questioner about greed, Jesus proceeded to tell what is popularly known as the parable of the rich fool. Let us look at it closely. A wealthy farmer had a bumper crop one year. He thought to himself, "What shall I do, for I have no place to store my crops?" Then he said, "I will do this: I will pull down my barns and build larger ones, and there I will store all my grain and my goods. And I will say to my soul, 'Soul, you have ample goods laid up for many years; relax, eat, drink, be merry.'" But God said to him, "You fool! This very night your life is being demanded of you. And the things you have prepared, whose will they be?" Jesus concluded by saying, "So it is with those who store up treasures for themselves but are not rich toward God."

Notice, first, the noun that God uses in this situation. He did not label this one as good or bad, but rather a "fool." Here was a man who was already rich, a farmer whose land brought forth in one season such an abundant harvest that he had no shelter big enough to house the surplus. So he decided that he would tear down what he had and make even greater provision to keep all the produce for himself. Having done that, he said confidently that now all his needs would be met forever, that he did not have to worry anymore, that he had provided for all eventualities. Now he could take his ease—eat, drink, and be merry—and forget about everything else.

It is precisely this kind of person that our culture often singles out as a real success. Yet Jesus, a Galilean peasant who had virtually nothing to call his own, declared this way of living profoundly foolish. Why do you think Jesus took such a position? I would like to suggest three possible clues.

First of all, the man was described as foolish because no amount of material wealth can give human beings security against all the uncertainties of our life. To put it simply, things can do only so much for you. We all have hungers and needs that no amount of wealth can touch. For example, money cannot make another person love or cherish you.

A few months ago I saw a rerun of that movie classic, *Citizen Kane*. One of the turning points occurs when the wife of the rich central figure announces that she has had enough and is going to leave him. He says, "But you can't," and she answers, "I am going to," and out she walks. There he was, in a magnificent estate surrounded by a whole cadre of servants. Yet for all that wealth and influence, he was powerless to make someone about whom he really cared remain by his side. You cannot force another to love you with money alone, nor can you forestall the approach of death. No matter how much you have, you cannot empower yourself to live forever. In this parable, Jesus affirms that our human hungers are of such a nature that there is only one resource that possesses all that we need, and that resource is the Holy One. If we build our hopes on anything other than the unfailing mercy of God, we will eventually find ourselves disappointed.

In another passage, Jesus speaks of building one's house upon either sand or a rock (Matthew 7:24-27). I invite you to think about the following possibilities in that light. If a doctor says to you that you have only two months to live, or your spouse tells you that he or she is leaving, you are likely to find yourself crumbling if your life has not been built on God's foundation. The rich fool was not evil, mind you. There is no hint that he made his fortune dishonestly. He was foolish, however, to think that wealth could do for him what in fact it did not have the power to do.

A second reason for describing this man as a fool is that he had missed the genuine delight that comes from an experience of profound gratitude, from realizing how much he had received that was utterly beyond his deserving. One of the highest of all joys lies in recognizing the primal grace behind all things. This farmer's egotism and lack of gratitude are awesome, indeed. Notice how often the words "I" and "my" occur in the story. Here is a man who obviously thought that his own efforts were the only source of the great bounty he had just harvested.

I heard once of an agronomist who used a computer to analyze all the components involved in the growing of a record wheat crop. His conclusion was that the universe provided about 95 percent of the energies required, while the farmer's energy accounted for only about 5 percent. When we consider the mysteries of rain and soil and seed and sunshine and the part they each play, it is almost comical to hear the farmer in the story speaking of "I" and "mine" as if his efforts had been the only factor in the abundant harvest. This is narcissism at its worst, and demonstrates how limited our vision can be.

Kentucky, the state of my birth, is technically called a "commonwealth," a term that recognizes the profound truth that all wealth is more of a social than an individual reality. No one can acquire nor maintain wealth apart from what others have done for us. Think of those who taught us how to read, write, compute, and work. One of the sterling joys of life is recognizing that we are playing just one instrument in a vast symphony of existence led by the Great Conductor. Here is occasion for real celebration! Behind all that we have lies a graciousness that cannot be measured, but is to be celebrated and acknowledged with genuine humility and gratitude. There is food for delight in simply being able to get up in the morning, in realizing that the world is still here, in having a measure of health and seeing the sun come up while the seasons move about us in their mysterious procession. There is much for which to be genuinely astonished and immeasurably grateful when mystery is your native home. The rich fool in our parable missed that point completely. His foolishness lay in his superficiality, his egotism, his lack of awareness and gratitude.

A third clue as to why the man was called foolish is found in his absence of generosity. I never tire of contending that generosity is the most basic of all the virtues. In the time before time, the Bible suggests that God said, "This wonder of aliveness is too good to keep to myself. I want others to get in on this ecstasy and to experience this wonder." This is the biblical answer to the question, "Why something and not nothing?" Creation is at bottom an act of generosity—God sharing the bounty of what he was and what he had—which is why the farmer in the parable is so out of touch with ultimate reality. He was foolish because he missed, by 180 degrees, what it means to be made in the image of God. He looked on his abundance and said the very opposite of what God said in the beginning. He proposed to keep it all to himself, which is the surest way to miss life's deepest meaning. Just as there is a delight in recognizing how much you have that you do not deserve or create, so there is another kind of delight—a kind of potency—that lies in seeing your generosity bless and energize other people. This quality of magnanimity lies at the root of our being the kind of creatures that we were meant to be.

Imagine, for a moment, that a neutron bomb has been dropped where you are. This particular weapon is the ultimate dream of the materialist, for it destroys human life but leaves all material things intact. Imagine that one of those bombs has been dropped in your area and by some unexplainable grace, you alone have been left to survive. There is not another human being anywhere around to prevent your taking possession of anything you want, for nobody else now lives in all the world.

Think of what that would be like! Any house that you want is yours to live in. Any car that you want to drive and any piece of jewelry you wish to wear can be yours, for there is no one to stand in your way of possessing anything your heart desires. Now, ask yourself if you could find joy in living in any house, or delight in driving any car, or exult in wearing any ring or owning any possession if there were no one else with whom to share these experiences? We are relational by nature and relational in our needs. It is a deep part of our essential humanity to be able to share what we are and what we have with someone else.

121

When God judged the man in our parable to be a fool, it must not have been with scorn but with infinite sadness, for he had missed what it means to be a human being. Perhaps the deepest sadness of this man was that he had not brought delight to others by what he had given to them. What a form of impoverishment indeed! Another facet of this same truth is that the clear differentiation between what one *is* and what one *has* gets acted out in the moment of death. We shall all be separated from the things we possess at that awesome juncture. To the rich man in the parable who hoarded all he owned for himself, Jesus posed this haunting question, "When you die, who will then own all this to which you are so attached?" My friend, death is going to make generous givers of us all. Everything we have will pass on to others eventually. "There are no pockets in a shroud," says an old Arab proverb, and most assuredly no way to take anything with you. So then, if we are made in the image of Generosity and if we are going to be generous ultimately, why not get in on the joy of participating intentionally in what is the very essence of our being?

There is an old story of a man who dreamed one night that he had died and was given a chance to visit both the underworld and the realm of heaven. In this dream, though, the one thing that death did to people was to stiffen their elbows: no one in either realm could bend their arms. In hell, the dreamer saw terrible conflict and agitation. Everyone had bread in both hands and was very hungry but, given the rigidity of their elbows, they could not get it to their mouths. Each one was concerned only for himself or herself, and the misery was unspeakable. The dreamer was then taken to heaven, where all the human beings had the same physical disability, only these folk had discovered a solution: although they could not feed themselves with the stiffened elbows, they could feed each other!

Generosity—a willingness to give—was finally the difference between heaven and hell, which is precisely the point Jesus was making in the parable of the rich fool.

Chapter Nine

THE PHARISEE AND THE PUBLICAN

He also told this parable to some who trusted in themselves that they were righteous and regarded others with contempt: "Two men went up to the temple to pray, one a Pharisee and the other a tax collector. The Pharisee, standing by himself, was praying thus, 'God, I thank you that I am not like other people: thieves, rogues, adulterers, or even like this tax collector. I fast twice a week; I give a tenth of all my income.' But the tax collector, standing far off, would not even look up to heaven, but was beating his breast and saying, 'God, be merciful to me, a sinner!' I tell you, this man went down to his home justified rather than the other; for all who exalt themselves will be humbled, but all who humble themselves will be exalted."

Luke 18:9-14

With the possible exception of the story of the good Samaritan, where a despised social outcast is depicted as morally superior to a priest and a Levite, no parable Jesus told could have been more shocking than this account of a Pharisee and a tax collector. The conclusion Jesus drew stood the conventional religious wisdom of that day on its ear. Yet through the details of the parable, a vision of the Holy One broke clear that is of great importance indeed. Therefore, let us look with care at this short but startling story.

All of those listening to Jesus would have been familiar with the Pharisees. These individuals were regarded as the most devout religious people in first-century Palestine. The name "Pharisee" derives from a root that means "pure." The Pharisees sought purity in all things—in the way they observed the law, in their unswerving nationalism, and in the care they took to avoid all contacts with the impure. They were a select and elite group—the very pillars of society—and on the side of righteousness in every situation.

In contrast, the tax collectors were at the opposite pole of the social strata. No other occupation was more despised or looked down upon. Whenever a country was conquered, the Romans recruited opportunistic local citizens to collect revenues. Obviously, this was a dirty business. Nobody likes to pay taxes under any circumstances, and certainly not to a kinsman who is working for the occupation forces. Individuals who stooped to this work were regarded as scoundrels and reprehensible traitors of the worst sort. What the term *quisling* (Nazi collaborator) came to mean in World War II conveys the kind of scorn tax collectors received in first-century

Palestine. They were the individuals for whom no decent human being had any respect.

It was no surprise to Jesus' audience, then, that a Pharisee had gone up to the temple to pray. Pharisees were famous for their religious enthusiasm, and the prayer that flowed from his lips exemplifies vintage Pharisaic piety. "God, I thank you that I am not like other men: thieves, rogues, adulterers, or even like this tax collector. I fast twice a week, I give a tenth of all my income." German scholar Joachim Jeremias has uncovered another first-century Pharisaic prayer that goes like this:

> I thank Thee, O Lord, my God, that Thou hath given me my right with those who sit in the seat of learning and not with those who sit on the street corners. Why, I am early to work and they are early to work, but I am early to work on the words of the Torah, and they are early to work on things that are of no moment. I weary myself—they weary themselves, but I weary myself and profit thereby—they weary themselves to no profit at all. I run, they run, but I run toward the Age to Come, they run towards the Pit of Destruction.

Jesus was not unfairly depicting the Pharisee in this story. The Pharisees believed they were morally superior to most other human beings and did not hesitate to apprise other people of this fact. There was no secret to the pride they had in themselves or their disdain of others.

The first element of surprise in the parable, then, lies not in the Pharisee's performance, but in the presence of the tax collector. As a rule, tax collectors did not frequent the temple precincts or demonstrate the kind of contrition that Jesus depicts here. This particular man remained a far way off, not even lifting his eyes to heaven, but beating his breast—the center of all decision making—saying simply, "God, be merciful to me, a sinner!" The image of a *repentant* tax collector defied all the stereotypes of the day.

However, imagine the earthquake of shock that must have followed Jesus' next statement: "I tell you, this man went down to his home justified rather than the other; for all who exalt themselves will be humbled, but all who humble themselves will be exalted." When Jesus said those words, I am confident a horrified gasp went up from all who were gathered to listen. To suggest that the God of all righteousness, the Creator of the universe, the Author of the Ten Commandments would be more pleased with a traitorous scoundrel than a person of moral rectitude was absolutely staggering in light of what the people had been taught all their lives. They probably could not believe their own ears. In effect, their conventional system of values was turned upside down!

This event reminds me of an incident I read about several years ago. A large New Jersey supermarket had recently converted to a system of computer labeling. All the clerks now had to do was run an item over a scanner that would automatically record the price. Some juvenile pranksters who knew a lot about computers, however, broke into the store and proceeded to change the prices on hundreds of items. They priced hams at twenty-five cents, for example, and a package of peas at twelve dollars. When the store opened the next morning and customers began to check out, total chaos ensued. The employees had to close the store in order to check every price for accuracy. The disruption of the relationship between price and value provides a modern parallel for the impact Jesus' parable must have made on the people who first heard it.

I want to pause and acknowledge that the shock those folk experienced as they listened to Jesus grew out of genuine moral concern. Was Jesus actually suggesting that it really did not matter what people did with their lives, or that one sort of behavior was no different from any other? A superficial understanding of this parable could lead to ethical chaos.

Take the Pharisee, for example. He says in all honesty, "I am not a thief, a rogue, or an adulterer." If we set aside for a moment the prejudices we have built up across the centuries, we might admit that the way this man depicts himself represents real moral achievement. Let's face it: to order one's business affairs along the lines of justice and honesty and one's personal interactions along the lines of non-exploitative chastity is no small accomplishment. Ask yourself, "If we did not have people like this Pharisee, how long could any society last? What permanence and stability would there be to any social fabric if there were not many folk who chose to use their power responsibly?"

The Pharisee goes on to report that he fasts twice a week and tithes a tenth of all his income. Helmut Thielicke, a wise German interpreter, says you can tell a person is serious about his or her religion when it affects two things: the stomach and the pocketbook.[1] We are all familiar with folk who turn to God when some crisis occurs. These are the people who become very religious only when they get to the end of their ropes.

It is something very different, however, when human beings allow their belief in God to affect the level of their bodily comfort. Fasting, you see, has never been a pleasant experience. It is somewhat akin to the discipline of training to be a marathon runner. These athletes do not just run when they feel like it: they keep to a regime whether it feels good or not, adding more and more distance as time goes by. Similarly, individuals who fast twice a week for religious reasons are not to be written off lightly: this discipline demands an extraordinary display of willpower.

The same can surely be said of the Pharisee's spiritual practice of tithing. Money, after all, is one of the most basic forms of potency available to human beings. It enables us to do and have any number of things, which is why it is such an ally to our egotism. If we control a lot of money, that means we possess the ability to have our own way in a variety of forms. To take that pool of power and voluntarily relinquish control over part of it out of loyalty to and affection for God is again a significant religious act. That the Pharisee offers a full ten percent of all he has to others is truly impressive.

Here was a person who was serious enough about God to let his devotion affect both his stomach and his pocketbook. For Jesus to suggest that this sort of person was religiously inferior to a man who had no spiritual track record at all, but in a moment of desperate crisis came begging for mercy was understandably upsetting. There is no indication in the parable that the tax collector intended to change his behavior or promised any reparation at all. He simply cried out for mercy in a time of need, which is religion of the most primitive, self-centered kind. It is no wonder that Jesus' hearers were aghast.

Do the Ten Commandments correspond to anything real? Are they actually "laws" like the law of gravity, descriptive of the way reality is put together—rules that cannot be broken without consequences?

Or is all of this fantasy? How could a man who had always been part of the problem and never part of the solution finally turn out to be more in favor with God than one who had taken morality seriously? We need to acknowledge the revolutionary and even threatening implications of Jesus' words here.

Helmut Thielicke warns that if we read this parable too superficially, the tax collector's humility could become the norm instead of the Pharisee's behavior. In fact, Thielicke composed a prayer that reflects this position:

> I thank Thee, God, that I am not as proud of myself as that Pharisee. To be sure, I am an extortioner. It is true, I am unjust and I am an adulterer, but that's what human beings are, and that is the way I am and at least I admit it. Therefore, because of my honesty, I think I am a little bit better than that other one. I commit fornication twice a week, I do not suppose over ten percent of what I get comes from honest work, but remember, I am being honest, God. I do not kid myself. I have no illusions about myself. Therefore, let your angels sing "Alleluia" over a sinner who is at least as honest as I am, willing to admit he is a dirty dog, and not trying to hide behind some kind of pretension like the Pharisee.[2]

There is something quite upsetting, to be sure, about making an admission of mediocrity into a virtue, about saying in effect, "I do not live by any high moral code, but neither does anyone else, so at least I'm not a hypocrite." If you have worked in the church for some time and have ever tried to get people involved in its affairs, you have certainly heard some people say, "Look, I am not a perfect person,

I do not claim to be, but at least I am not a hypocrite like all those churchgoers."

In the parish I served in Kentucky several years ago, there was a remarkable man named John, somewhat limited in his mental development, but very devout and willing to serve the church in every way. During a visitation campaign one fall, this man volunteered to call on prospects for the church. We were a bit uncertain what to do, but finally sent him out with an experienced church worker who returned with a memorable account. They had called on an individual who said heatedly, "I am not going to go to church because it's nothing but a bunch of hypocrites," to which John replied, "Well, come on down, there is always room for one more."

Seriously, though, there is something frightening about letting moral carelessness become the accepted norm. It is very important that we look more deeply at this parable and steer clear of the conclusion that the moral values that we have always held dear are of no consequence at all. I am convinced Jesus was making a different point in this parable. What, then, does this story mean?

Obviously, this Pharisee had reached a high level of moral maturity. He had established control over his physical impulses and was the master of his money rather than allowing his money to be master over him. In his journey from birth to the ideal, however, he had made a fatal mistake: he took his eyes off the goal at the end of the process, that completeness that is the high calling of God. He began to compare himself to the people alongside him rather than to the true Omega Point out ahead.

Two devastating effects followed this shift of focus: the Pharisee grew proud of himself and the level to which he had risen and complacent about the distance he still had to grow toward the ultimate goal of maturity. It was as if the Pharisee were a tenth-grader comparing himself to a student in the second grade. Jesus used this example to show that when our focus is deflected from the Holy One, our growth into spiritual maturity is dealt a lethal blow. The old question, "Compared to what?" is really crucial at this point. In any developmental endeavor, the place where we choose to fix our focus is all-important. A sidelong glance is very different from fixing our attention on the ultimate goal. When our concentration is broken, the results can be devastating.

Illustrations of this truth are all around us. If you follow any kind of sports very carefully, you know how important it is to keep your eye on the ball. Again and again in football, someone fails to catch a pass. "He started to run before the ball got there," the commentator will say. "He did not watch it all the way into his hands." This means he let something besides the ultimate goal deflect his attention.

Dr. Thielicke, quoted earlier in the chapter, was the chaplain of the University of Hamburg during the terrible rise and fall of the Third Reich in Germany. At the end of the war he agonized with his fellow countrymen over all the chaos they had helped to bring on the whole world. He noted that had the Germans stayed focused on "the beam in their own eye," real moral renewal might have followed World War II. Somehow, however, the focus shifted, and the Germans began to say, "But the British, the French, the Russians, and the Dutch are not all perfect either." Before long, the desire for moral regeneration began to weaken. This happens every time we start looking *around* instead of *ahead,* for the energies to grow are kept alive by focusing on the ultimate goal.

I experienced this same loss of focus some years ago when I made the transition from the Baptist ministry into the Episcopal priesthood. In the year I spent in an Episcopal seminary, my goal was to learn the many things about liturgy, church history, and sacramental theology that were basic to competence in my newly chosen vocational niche. I threw myself into this period of "Anglicizing" with great energy. Late one afternoon, I was working away at my desk in the library when a classmate of mine in Liturgics 303 came by.

"You are really working late," he said.

"I am trying to finish this reading assignment for liturgics class tomorrow," I replied.

"Don't you realize the teacher assigns more than anybody is expected to read? He means for you to use the next five years to get through all that material. Nobody else in the class is reading that much. You are taxing yourself unduly." And with that, he walked on.

I pondered his words. I had assumed that assignments were assignments, that everybody was doing what the teacher had prescribed. With that, I closed my book and went home to watch television.

The next morning in liturgics class, we came to a point that was very important, something I wanted and needed to know. The teacher reminded us that it was addressed in the assigned reading section for that day. No one in the class had read it. We were all caught "off base," and it suddenly dawned on me that I had let what other people were doing deflect me from the goal that had brought me to the seminary in the first place. I was not there to conform to the practices of other students, but to learn all I could about areas that were going to be essential to my future ministry. I had made the same mistake as this Pharisee, the football player, and the German people: I had substituted the sidelong glance for a clear focus on my ultimate goal and thereby thwarted the impulse to grow. This is what Jesus was criticizing in the Pharisee—not what he had achieved, but how he had taken his eye off the goal.

133

The tax collector, on the other hand, was in a very different position. He had achieved nothing, really, in the sphere of moral development. He was in kindergarten, you might say, in terms of what God wanted him to be, but something had happened in his life to jog him awake. Here he was, honestly acknowledging his lack and crying out for grace to help him in his time of trouble.

We are not told by Jesus what it was that had brought this man to his senses and to his knees. However, one of the ways that God's ingenious grace often works is to let us, in freedom, misuse our power and make an absolute mess of our own and others' lives. This usually creates a great deal of suffering through which, like the prodigal son, we sometimes "come to ourselves" and realize how far we are from the goal God originally intended for us.

I have seen this happen again and again and again. In a little country church where I served early in my career, there was a man who was a hardworking tenant farmer. Most of the time he was a respected citizen, a faithful husband, and a good father, but he had an erratic drinking problem. He could go for six months and be dry as a bone, and then something would snap inside. He would go on a binge and spend all the family money and become physically abusive to his wife and children.

I had prayed for this man and talked to him directly about his situation many times, but somehow, the gospel never seemed to get through to him.

Then late one Saturday night, I received a call to go to their house. Upon my arrival, I discovered that he had been on his worst binge ever. Something his wife had said upset him, and he responded by beating her savagely.

134

That event finally brought him to his senses. He suddenly saw the face of his own wife bleeding because of his violence. The horror of what he had done came home to him so powerfully in that moment that he cried out, "I have got to have help. I want to be different. I must ask a Power into my life to change me." That was when he called for me, and the moment marked the beginning of a healing process. I took him to an Alcoholics Anonymous group in a nearby town and connected him with some people who knew how to deal with his illness. He began to discover God's help in very tangible ways and to move in a new direction.

In all likelihood, the tax collector had had a similar experience—some event that made him aware of how out of sync with his true self he actually was. The very first of the famous Twelve Steps in AA is admitting that your life is out of control and that on your own you do not have the power to correct things. This is precisely what that tax collector was admitting in the temple. Jesus saw that while he had achieved very little, the tax collector had at last assumed the stance that held the promise for growth. This is possible when we honestly acknowledge where we are, horrible as that may be, and accept the fact that there is One bigger than we are who is willing to help.

Our sins and lack of achievement are not the only realities on the stage of history. There is also the reality of God's everlasting mercy and unending patience—God's desire, no matter what, to bring us to full completion. When grace of this sort is given access to our lives, as seems to be the case with the tax collector, then the possibility for spiritual growth is enhanced.

Can you imagine the Pharisee, having thus shifted his focus, coming out of the temple with a desire to move deeper into God's ultimate fullness? Can you imagine him saying, "There are areas where I yet must grow and need God to help me"? Of course not. Pride in himself and contempt for others had served to knock him completely off stride in a race he had not yet completed. He had taken his eyes off the proper goal of human existence.

It is not hard, however, to conceive of the tax collector leaving the temple in such a creative and hopeful frame of mind. He had broken through in his honesty to the one thing that is utterly essential to completion: the availability of the divine grace that enables the whole process. By looking forward to the goal of God's grace, not sideways at the others with him, the tax collector rather than the Pharisee "went to his home justified."

In conclusion, then, let me review what each of us can take away from this story to inspire our own growth. Parables, remember, are about us, not about others. They are mirrors—not portraits of other people.

First of all, the issue here is attitude, not achievement. I am sure Jesus felt both glad and sad for each one of these men, but in opposite ways. He was glad for the Pharisee in terms of what he had accomplished, but sad that he had lost his focus and had become complacent in his self-righteousness. On the other hand, he was sad for the tax collector's past and all the opportunities he had lost, but glad that at last he had "seen the light" and was committed to growing. Given their present attitudes, the Pharisee had a past but no future, while the tax collector had the opposite—no past to brag about, but a genuine promise of a better future.

With God, the future is always more significant than the past. The Holy One is more interested in what we can become than in what we used to be. It is not God's nature to hold the past against us when we set out with him to become new creatures. Jesus' point here is not one of moral relativity, as if it does not matter how we live or what we do. It is rather that our attitude toward God's grace is the thing that is most important.

My second point is that the criteria we select to evaluate our lives are equally crucial. "Compared to what?" is the basic question in any act of interpretation. Jesus is reminding us here that what other people are doing or failing to do is beside the point. God created us to participate in the divine life and to experience fully divine joy. That is our true reason for being and the goal toward which all existence moves. The Good News is that the One who began such a sharing has the ability and the mercy and the patience to achieve this end. God promises, "You shall be perfect by my grace, if you will only allow me."

My third point is simply to note that what happened to the Pharisee is a special temptation for those who have achieved a high level of moral development. The very people who have the capacity to fast and to tithe, who by hard and rigorous effort have made something significant of themselves, have a greater temptation to take their eyes off the goal. Someone has said that burnout is a major problem in our society because it tends to affect the most conscientious and useful citizens. The homeless man on an urban street corner is not vulnerable to this kind of burnout. It is the president of the Chamber of Commerce, the individual who serves on six or eight boards, or the person who really does want to be part of the answer and not part of the problem who are the ones most at risk.

In the same way, those who are really serious about their religion and want to become the kind of person that God wants them to be are the ones most in danger. They can get "halfway home," only to start looking around and seeing all the rascals and scalawags who are not doing half as much, and grow complacent. For such folk, it is doubly important to keep their eyes fixed on god's mercy—the ultimate hope of the task being completed. Perfection, remember, comes as promise, not as some achievement we create on our own. We shall become full grown by God's grace, and God's grace alone. There is no other way.

My last point is that we are not to judge others. If our reading of this parable has been correct—that we are to keep our true focus—then it is not up to us to judge where other people are, how they are doing, or what their level of spiritual development might be. For one thing, this is an area where we simply do not have enough evidence upon which to base a judgment. None of us ever knows enough about another to render an accurate verdict.

My wife and I were listening to a tape the other night in which a Roman Catholic priest asked these interesting questions. "Have any of you ever seen a motive? Do you really know all the reasons why a person does what that one does?" The answer, of course, is "No." We simply do not know what kind of things have happened and are happening in other people's lives.

I have a friend who once was in a particularly angry stage of his life. He was the leader of a church where there were lots of problems. He had a dream one night, during which Jesus came to him and said, "Harry, I am not pleased with your ministry these days. I have been listening to your sermons, and you sound more like the public prosecutor than the public defender. You are so judgmental and critical and harsh with your folk."

"But, Lord, I cannot justify what some of my people are doing," he replied.

"Whoever asked you to justify them? That's my job. All I have asked you to do is to love those folk, to forgive them, to wash their feet and nurture them."

My friend woke up and let the truth of that dream impact his life. He realized that he had gotten off the track of his true calling. "There and then," he later told me, "I shifted the focus of my ministry from the judge's bench to the basin and the towel. Instead of asking 'Where did you get your feet dirty, or why did you not keep yourself more clean,' I resolved simply to deal with their dirt as Jesus dealt with mine." He now reports that the joy of being a minister has begun to return.

Remember, we never know enough about other people to judge them. Since we did not create these folk, we are not ultimately responsible for them. That is God's job, and God is more than up to the task. It would be easy to look cynically at this tax collector and say, "I'll bet this is just another manipulative ploy, another con job," but we have no right to do that. God knows—of that we can be sure. In *The Book of Common Prayer* we pray: "Almighty God, to you all hearts are open, all desires known, and from you no secrets are hid." We can trust that

the One who saw deep into the heart of that tax collector perceived his real desire to change and his willingness to receive the divine help he needed to grow.

There is much beyond our present grasp to which
we yet aspire. We have all fallen short of what we
were meant to be, yet there is something bigger than
our past or our sin, and that something is the grace
of God. If we keep our eyes fixed on that goal and
on that grace, we will, on the authority of God's
promise, finally arrive at home!

139

Chapter Ten

THE FINAL
JUDGMENT

*When the Son of Man comes in his glory, and all the
angels with him, then he will sit on the throne of his
glory. All the nations will be gathered before him,
and he will separate people one from another as a
shepherd separates the sheep from the goats, and he
will put the sheep at his right hand, and the goats at
the left. Then the king will say to those at his right
hand, "Come, you that are blessed by my Father,
inherit the kingdom prepared for you from the
foundation of the world; for I was hungry and you
gave me food, I was thirsty and you gave me something to drink, I was a stranger and you welcomed
me, I was naked and you gave me clothing, I was
sick and you took care of me, I was in prison and
you visited me." Then the righteous will answer
him, "Lord, when was it that we saw you hungry
and gave you food, or thirsty and gave you something to drink? And when was it that we saw you a
stranger and welcomed you, or naked and gave you*

clothing? And when was it that we saw you sick or in prison and visited you?" And the king will answer them, "Truly I tell you, just as you did it to one of the least of these who are members of my family, you did it to me."

141

Then he will say to those at his left hand, "You that are accursed, depart from me into the eternal fire prepared for the devil and his angels; for I was hungry and you gave me no food, I was thirsty and you gave me nothing to drink, I was a stranger and you did not welcome me, naked and you did not give me clothing, sick and in prison and you did not visit me." Then they also will answer, "Lord, when was it that we saw you hungry or thirsty or a stranger or naked or sick or in prison, and did not take care of you?" Then he will answer them, "Truly, I tell you, just as you did not do it to one of the least of these, you did not do it to me." And these will go away into eternal punishment, but the righteous into eternal life.

Matthew 25:31-46

If I had to pick the three most influential parables that Jesus ever told, I would have to include this story of the final judgment as described in Matthew's gospel. In my opinion, no set of images Jesus ever used has shaped Western civilization more profoundly. The statement "Just as you did it to one of the least of these. . . , you did it to me" has found its way into many places and has been highly significant in the formation of Christian behavior. Here is one of Jesus' most powerful truths, and for that reason we need to look at it most carefully.

It would be very easy to read this parable and miss the gospel. In fact, many people have done just that and reduced Christian faith to nothing more than a call for humanitarian activity. They have turned Christian salvation into something one earns by virtue of how much good one does. For this reason, it is important that we not fall prey to such a misreading of this important part of Jesus' teaching.

Here, as always, our Lord took some familiar first-century Palestinian images and used them, first to intrigue his hearers, then at the proper moment to surprise them by revealing something they very much needed to learn. Please keep in mind that Jesus lived in an agricultural society, where growing food and taking care of animals were the main ways of earning a living. In that era, sheep and goats ate the same kind of grass, so it was quite common for one shepherd to have both as part of his flock. At sundown, however, all of that changed, for the two species of animals had different nighttime needs. Goats did not have very thick hair, which meant they needed shelter to protect them against the chill of the night air, while sheep were covered with a heavy coat of wool and could easily spend the night in the open. Separating the sheep from the goats was relatively easy, moreover, because Palestinian goats were usually black but sheep were usually white. There were some exceptions, of course, but it was not that hard, even in the deepening shadows, to distinguish one from the other

The two species had differing economic values as well. Sheep were capable of producing a coat of wool which could be sheared and sold each year; then, after many seasons of that kind of production, they were slaughtered and sold for food. Goats, on the other hand, had much less economic value: only their milk produced a profit. It follows, then, that much more attention was paid to sheep than to goats, and the task of separating them from each other at the end of the day was a common procedure.

Jesus took this familiar pastoral practice and used it as an analogy for what is going to happen when the sun goes down on history; that is, at the end of time. His metaphor for this event is, "When the Son of Man comes in his glory." C. S. Lewis contends that if you know much about the theater, you realize that when the author steps on the stage, the play is over! In this parable, the Author of history comes on stage and proceeds to bring all that has been said and done to a climax. To use a contemporary image, at the sunset of history there is going to be a final examination of all of us—an accounting of what we have done with our days and our nights. Such an awesome conclusion to history is the point of this parable.

Before we examine the particulars of this story, let me ask you honestly: How does the prospect of some being sent to the right and some to the left make you feel? Here again, Jesus asserts that human existence is a decisive affair: we *do* have choices, and real consequences grow out of how we exercise our freedom. I think Jesus is warning us that ultimate failure is a possibility, that nothing is automatic in our kind of world.

I do not see how we can read this parable and not sense that Jesus is alerting us to the fact that our existence has a decisive character, and what we choose to do makes a difference. Our lives really are headed somewhere. This world is not a fool's paradise where no matter what we do, it will all come out the same. What we do or fail to do is a crucial component in the shaping of our destiny. It is not the only factor, thanks be to God, but it is a crucial one.

Across the centuries, real effort has been expended to soften the implications of these last two assertions.

Some say that even though human existence is decisive, God's grace is so powerful and ingenious that failure and tragedy are not ultimate possibilities: somehow grace will win out and everything will end on a totally positive note. The theological word for this position is "universalism." It means that in the end every person will finally be saved and every creature will be brought back home to God.

There is no question that certain verses in the scriptures seem to support such an optimistic view. For example, Jesus did not condemn the world when he died but instead spoke merciful words: "Father, forgive them; for they do not know what they are doing." In John's gospel, Jesus is remembered as having said, "And I, when I am lifted up from the earth, will draw all people to myself" (12:32). In other words, what Jesus has done through his costly act of love will have a redemptive impact on every person.

Paul picks up this note and in some of his writings appears to embrace universalism. "For as all die in Adam," he says, "so all will be made alive in Christ" (1 Corinthians 15:22). In his letter to the Philippians, Paul quotes a hymn that was popular in the first century: "At the name of Jesus every knee should bend...and every tongue should confess that Jesus Christ is Lord" (Philippians 2:10-11). Again, in his Corinthian correspondence, Paul says that in the end death, the last enemy of God, will be overcome. All evil will be swallowed up and God will become all in all, everything to everyone (1 Corinthians 15:26-28). So there are several portions of scripture that affirm that grace is going to triumph, and the ingenious mercy of God is going to win back every creature.

Let me say that I hope with all my heart that this is true. If the final outcome of history is totally positive, and no part of creation is left out, I will be totally delighted! However, if we take seriously the whole sweep of the biblical vision, I simply do not see how we can say dogmatically, "This is the way it is going to come out."

There are two powerful reasons for my skepticism: our God-given freedom and the nature of God's love. If human freedom is genuine and God really does give us autonomy when we are called into being, and if love is not coercive, how can we unequivocally assert that everybody is going to behave a certain way? Grace is not a bulldozer that finally makes people do something, whether they are willing or not. I hope with all my heart that love finds a way to woo freely every single soul back to God. Yet to assert dogmatically that this *has* to happen seems to go against the grain, not only of this parable, but of the whole tenor of Holy Scripture. "Choose this day whom you will serve" (Joshua 24:15) is a meaningless imperative if human beings have no freedom, or if God is finally going to force us to end up at a certain place. Universalism may be a more loving form of determinism than predestination, but it is still determinism. Such a view does violence to the mystery of both the divine and the human as they are depicted in the biblical vision.

If a human being fails to reach the goal God wants, who is to blame? Once again, the biblical witness is complex and multifaceted. Certain portions of Holy Scripture seem to imply that God has a limited amount of mercy and patience. If humans continue to thwart him, the Holy One finally "gives up" and proceeds understandably to blow up in frustration over our unwillingness to let God have his way with us. The problem in this approach is both human intractability and the limited supply of God's mercy.

146

Matthew 18:14 is my North Star when I search for my theological bearings: "It is not the will of your Father in heaven that one of these little ones should be lost." What God creates, God loves; and what God loves, God loves everlastingly. Therefore, if there is an ultimate failure, I do not think we can rightly lay the charge at God's feet—except to acknowledge that God is the One who gave us freedom in the first place and set this whole adventure into motion. No, if there is ultimate failure it can better be traced back to our own freedom and unwillingness to say "yes" to the gift of existence—the very chance to be alive—that God gives us. You see, if there is nothing about life that pleases me—my body, my mind, or any of the opportunities that are before me—then there is nothing even an omnipotent God can do to alter such negativity.

You may be familiar with the work of Jean-Paul Sartre, the French existentialist who wrote extensively in the mid-twentieth century. Toward the end of his life he wrote an autobiography entitled *Nausea*. After reflecting upon all his days and nights, his ultimate reaction was, "The whole thing makes me want to throw up!" This was his final estimate of life in all its facets.[1] Sheer brute force is powerless, therefore, to create joy in people of such a mindset.

I have referred before to C. S. Lewis's observation that either we say to God, "Your will be done," and enter into divine joy, or God says these same words to us and with infinite sadness lets us go back into the nothingness from whence we came. This would be an eternal punishment, but not an eternal punishing. If a creature called into existence by God says, "I do not want to live; I don't like anything about life," it is inconceivable to me that God would continue to hold this soul in an existence of unending torture and pain. No decent human being would even treat a dog like that. Therefore, I do not believe God is going to subject people forever to senseless torture simply out of frustration.

I do think, however, that if we have said in a million ways, "I do not want to be—I don't want to have anything to do with the gift of existence as you are giving it," even God will realize that he does not have the power to make us experience joy. This is why letting us go back into the nothingness from which we came is the only compassionate solution. God will always remember sadly, "I wanted that person to know my infinite joy, but even I cannot force this attitude on another."

It is instructive to remember how Jesus said from the depths of his heart:

> Jerusalem, Jerusalem…! How often have I desired to gather your children together as a hen gathers her brood under her wings, and you were not willing! (Matthew 23:37)

There will always be grief in the heart of God over our unwillingness to accept the gift of life, but such a reality can only be willingly received. It cannot be injected like a shot of penicillin.

How does this perspective square with the image at the end of the parable of the talents: the slave being sentenced to "the outer darkness, where there will be weeping and gnashing of teeth" (Matthew 25:30)? I think this passage refers not to some punishment that is inflicted upon us after death, but to the quality of experience that results from disliking every aspect of God's gift to us. If nausea is our primary metaphor for life, then that is compatible with the images of anguish in the parable. Notice carefully, however, that this state of being does not grow out of God's vindictive nature, but out of our decision to dislike life the way it is. This is not what God desires for us: if such anguish occurs, it will be literally "over God's dead body"—in the action of Jesus on the cross, when love did everything love is capable of doing. To coerce would be to violate the very nature of love, and this God will not do.

Let me stress that God does not want a tragic destiny for anyone, and this parable is one of the strategies that Jesus employs to help us choose another way. In a sense, Jesus is giving us the final exam in the middle of the course. He is telling us in advance, "This is what is going to be most important in the end." Perhaps we will then get the point, and use our freedom to opt for joy.

One of the finest professors I ever had taught Greek and Latin at Baylor University. A learned man, he had a passion to communicate what he knew to others. After preparing us thoroughly, he would give us a test on the material. When we finished, we would bring our test up to his desk, and he would proceed to grade it right there as we sat beside him. I can still see his red pencil marking each mistake, but his involvement did not stop there. He used that occasion to teach us the right answer. You see, his purpose was not simply to give out grades or to flunk a struggling student. He was there to share the wonder and wisdom of an ancient language, and even the act of testing was a mechanism for teaching.

It is in this sense that we can best understand the parable of the last judgment. Jesus is giving us the final exam well in advance, precisely because he wants us to pass it with flying colors. Its purpose is not to condemn us, but to give us a sense of where we are in our own development and how we need to grow. The purpose of this parable is not to scare the hell out of us, but rather to inspire us to grow in the direction of heavenly joy.

What, then, is the continuum of perfection or wholeness that underlies our human existence? What would it mean to move step by step toward the kind of fulfillment that God desires for each one of us? The biblical vision, it seems to me, is centered in the reality of love, and we need to consider very carefully the precise nature of this reality.

In one of his last books, *The Four Loves,* C. S. Lewis makes a clear distinction between what he calls "need-love" and "gift-love." Need-love is something that is born of emptiness, something that is always on the lookout for values outside itself that can fill it. This kind of love involves seeing something in another person that is highly appealing and immediately reaching out to possess it. Need-love is by nature a circular affair—it goes out of itself for the purpose of returning to itself with whatever has been gained. It is always acquisitive: its goal is to get something for itself. The transfer of value is always from the object to the subject.

Lewis observes that much of what goes on in the name of love is actually this sort of transaction. When a person says, "I love you," they may well be saying, "I need you, I want you, I desire to take something of what you are to fill the emptiness inside myself." Think of the times we have all loved something because the beloved had a value we wanted to acquire. Who can claim to be a complete stranger to this form of loving?

Alongside need-love, however, Lewis describes a very different sort of reality called gift-love. It belongs on the opposite end of the continuum, for instead of being born of emptiness, it is born of fullness. Instead of reaching out to get, this kind of love reaches out to give. Instead of being a circle that goes out only to return to the source, gift-love is an arc—it flows out simply to confer value, not to extract it. If the transfer of value in need-love is from object to subject, with gift-love the transfer is from subject to object. Its sole agenda is to enhance the value of the beloved, not to acquire value from the beloved. If a vacuum is a natural symbol for need-love, an over-flowing artesian well is the symbol for gift-love. It is essentially creative rather than extractive, the epitome of generosity rather than exploitation.

Once we have this distinction clearly in mind, Lewis says that the best way to sum up the essence of the Christian vision is to say that God's love is gift-love, not need-love.[2] God's reason for creating was to give something of himself, not to get something. There was no self-emptiness that the Holy One attempted to fill by making the world. Rather, there was an ampleness that made God overflow. The deepest truth of the gospel is that this is who God is and that we are made in the image of such a One.

When we apply such a vision to the images in this parable, they begin to come to life in a beautiful and inspiring way For example, the king says to all of those on the right:

> Come, you that are blessed by my Father, inherit the kingdom prepared for you from the foundation of the world; for I was hungry and you gave me food, I was thirsty and you gave me something to drink, I was a stranger and you welcomed me, I was naked and you gave me clothing, I was sick and you took care of me, I was in prison and you visited me.

Here were people who did not possess any notable value: the hungry, the thirsty, the naked, and the sick.

They had little to offer—if getting something back were the motive of the blessed ones on the right.

However, since the blessed ones knew that they were made in the image of gift-love, like artesian wells they overflowed freely and joyfully and transferred some of their value over to those who really needed it. Their goal was to enhance those struggling people, not to exploit them. Because they were utterly unself-conscious in what they were doing, it is clear that they were operating out of a gift-love stance. When Jesus explained to them why they were inheriting the kingdom, they were amazed, and in their response it was clear that they had not been trying to gain anything by what they did. This is why the king replied, in today's idiom, "That is precisely the point. You were doing what you were doing because of who you are, not to get something for yourself." We come to the goal that God wants for everyone by realizing that we are the sons and daughters of gift-love itself. We do not do the acts described in the parable to earn God's love. We do them finally because that is who we are—it is our true nature to give such love.

Visiting a hospital the other day, I saw a beautiful little girl running ahead of her parents down the hall. Somehow she fell and cut her chin open as she hit a flower pot. She immediately began to cry in great anguish. The three of us who were actually closer to her than her parents instinctively stooped over to do what we could to help. Her parents came right behind, of course, and took her to get the wound sewn up. My point is, the instinct to help that stricken child came perfectly naturally because there was no overlay of fear or prejudice. This is the way we humans act in the face of need when our true natures are at work. Gift-love is our birthright if only we will claim it!

Look now at those on the left hand, however. They confronted the same conditions as those on the right, yet they chose to do nothing. The hungry, the thirsty, the naked, the sick, the imprisoned—those on the left were indifferent to them because these individuals had nothing to offer in terms of value or appeal. Here is the reality of need-love at work. The true nature of those on the left came out when the king said, "I was hungry and you gave me no food, I was thirsty and you gave me nothing to drink," and so forth. These folk were aghast. They asked, in contemporary wording, "When, O Mighty One, did we see you in need and pass up a chance to manipulate you and get in good with you? Had we known the King of the universe was near, you can bet your last dollar we would have done something." But that was just the point—they were still stuck in need-love. This kind of self-serving behavior is literally "falling short of the glory," which is how the apostle Paul defines the essence of sin. The old Hebrew image is that of "missing the mark," of not yet being what we are meant to be.

The whole point of Jesus giving us the final exam in the middle of the course is not to frighten us into failure, but to inspire us to recognize and begin to actualize our true identities. The purpose of this parable is not to scare us into contriving a lot of humanitarian acts in order selfishly to acquire salvation. If we start feeding the hungry and clothing the naked simply to gain a reward, we have missed the whole point. Jesus came to change the way we understand ourselves and our relationship to God. The most important truth of all is this: God's love is gift-love, not need-love, and we are made in the image of that reality. There is an artesian well in everyone whose source is the abundance of God. We are what we are because of who our Parent is, and once this identity becomes deeply rooted in our being, then an unself-conscious giving of self will become a way of life. This is another way of saying that we "inherit the kingdom prepared for us from the foundation of the world."

The proper application of this parable, then, is to ask, "Where am I on this continuum of need-love and gift-love? Am I still mired down in the illusion of not-enoughness and therefore seeking to use everyone in sight to fill my emptiness?" That is why those on the left paid no attention to the needy ones: they were fixated on their own emptiness and using all their energies to acquire for themselves. The truth of the matter is that such self-concern is unnecessary. We already are fulfilled, not by virtue of what we have to make of ourselves, but by virtue of what God has made of us. All that we need has already been deposited in us by the grace of creation. Therefore, the kind of behavior that evoked Jesus' praise—"I was hungry and you gave me food, I was thirsty and you gave me something to drink"—is not some kind of manipulative ploy. This parable is about identity, finally, and not about surface behavior.

There is a medieval fable that describes a mother tiger who died giving birth to a cub. This meant the newly-born creature was without any support as he wandered through the forest. A pack of goats came upon the little tiger and, sensing his plight, invited him to join their company. As the months went by, this creature gradually took on all the qualities of a goat, even though he was by nature a tiger.

One day the king tiger, happening through the same forest, saw the tiger cub acting like a silly goat and roared out, "What is the meaning of this unseemly masquerade? Why are you behaving in such a way?" All the cub knew was to bleat nervously and begin to nibble grass. Then it dawned on the king tiger what the problem was: this little creature had no idea who he was.

The older animal took the little one down to a river and let him see for the first time a reflection of himself. "See," the king tiger said. "You are not really a goat, you are one of us." Then he laid back his head and let the creature hear how a tiger was suppose to sound. At that juncture, the king tiger said, "Follow me, little one, and I will help you become the grand thing you already have it in you to be!"

This fable allegedly inspired T. S. Eliot to refer once to "Christ, The Tiger." Is there any wonder? Jesus came among us as the embodiment of all that God ever intended human beings to be. He said, "Follow me, and I will enable you to become the same grand thing!" By showing us our true natures, Jesus opens the way for us to become authentic and complete.

Where, then, are you on this continuum of becoming? Gift-love is your inheritance. Why not claim it now joyfully?

ENDNOTES

CHAPTER ONE
1. Kyle Haselden, *Flux and Fidelity* (Richmond, Va.: John Knox Press, 1968)
2. C. S. Lewis, *The Great Divorce* (New York: Macmillan, 1946).
3. Raymond Moody, *Life After Life* (New York: Bantam Starfire, 1988).

CHAPTER THREE
1. Geddes MacGregor, *He Who Lets Us Be: A Theology of Love* (St. Paul, Minn.: Paragon House, 1987).
2. C. S. Lewis, *The Weight of Glory and Other Sermons* (New York: Touchstone Books, 1996).
3. M. Scott Peck, *The Road Less Traveled* (New York: Simon & Schuster, 1978, 1985), 272.
4. Bob Benson, *Laughter in the Walls* (Nashville: Impact Books, 1969).

CHAPTER FOUR

1. Harold S. Kushner, *When Bad Things Happen to Good People* (New York: Schocken Books, 1981).

2. Ibid.

3. A homily by Eduard Richard Riegert from *The Lutheran Quarterly,* vol.16 (February, 1974).

CHAPTER FIVE

1. Karen Horney, "Neurosis and Human Growth," *Concepts of Personality,* ed. Ralph Heine and Joseph Wepman (New York: W. W. Norton, 1991).

2. Ibid.

3. Ibid., 86.

4. Agnes Sanford, *The Healing Light* (St. Paul, Minn.: Macalester Park, 1947).

5. Sam Keen, *To a Dancing God* (New York: Harper & Row, 1970).

6. James Finley, *Merton's Palace of Nowhere* (Notre Dame, Ind.: Ave Maria Press, 1978).

CHAPTER EIGHT

1. Peter deVries, *The Mackeral Plaza* (Boston: Little, Brown, 1958).

CHAPTER NINE

1. Helmut Thielicke, *The Waiting Father: Sermons on the Parables of Jesus* (New York: Harper, 1959).

2. Ibid., 129.

CHAPTER TEN

1. Jean Paul Sartre, *Nausea* (Norfolk, Conn.: New Direction, 1964).

2. C. S. Lewis, *The Four Loves* (New York: Harcourt, Brace, 1960).